The Saga of
Hanumān

A Universally Venerated Deity

Amb. Dr. Prakash Joshi

**MOTILAL BANARSIDASS
INTERNATIONAL
DELHI**

First Edition : Delhi, 2026

© Motilal Banarsidass International
All Rights Reserved

ISBN : 978-93-47683-03-9

Also available at :

MOTILAL BANARSIDASS INTERNATIONAL

41 U.A. Bungalow Road, (Back Lane) Jawahar Nagar, Delhi-110007
4261/3 (Basement), Ansari Road, Darya Ganj, New Delhi-110002
Shop#. 6, 241, Luz Ginza Complex, Luz Corner, Mylapore, Chennai - 600004
12/1A, 2nd Floor, Bankim Chatterjee Street, Kolkata - 700073

Stockist : Motilal Books, Ashok Rajpath, Near Kali Mandir, Patna-800004

Printed in India by
MOTILAL BANARSIDASS INTERNATIONAL

Dedication

To
My beloved Mother

Manik Joshi

Who always asked me to be mindful of Dharma,

And to countless devotees of Lord Hanumān who always chant
Hanumān Chālīsā

A Timeless Ideal of Divinity

In the vast tapestry of Hindu tradition, Hanuman Ji occupies a unique and cherished space. He is the divine being who shows us the path from the restless, impulsive mind (symbolized by the monkey) to the highest state of spiritual evolution. His journey is our journey-a testament to what can be achieved through perseverance, discipline and most importantly, absolute and selfless devotion. For millennia, the figure of Hanuman has captivated hearts and minds across the Indian subcontinent and beyond. He is more than a powerful warrior or a loyal companion; he is the ultimate expression of the divine potential residing within a humble and surrendered heart.

The author has focused on the unique position of Hanuman Ji as a being who transcends human and animal forms to embody the highest divine virtues. The unparalleled devotion of Hanuman Ji to Lord Rama, his immense strength and wisdom has been emphasized that reveals profound spiritual lessons. This book is an exploration of the profound truth that Hanuman's divinity is not something external or unattainable, but a reflection of the highest human potential. He is often depicted with a heart open, revealing the presence of Lord Rama and Sita. The image is not merely symbolic; it teaches us that the divine resides within the heart of every true devotee. This book is a profound journey into the very essence of that divinity, exploring why Hanuman Ji is revered as a god in his own right, an incarnation of Lord Shiva, and the perfect devotee of Lord Rama.

While The Ramayana highlights Hanuman's extraordinary feats-leaping oceans, lifting mountains, and vanquishing powerful demons- his true divinity lies not in these acts of immense power, but in the perfect balance of strength, humility, and wisdom he embodies. His life teaches us that true power is found not in ego, but in selfless service and unwavering faith. He is the embodiment of the truth that even the impossible becomes possible when we act as an instrument of the divine. By meditating on his qualities, we are reminded to cultivate inner strength, quiet the restless mind, and dedicate our actions to a higher purpose.

This work is an invitation lo readers to look past the stories and embrace the divine qualities that Hanuman personifies. This book seeks to reveal the spiritual lessons contained within each of his legendary stories. It presents Hanuman not just as a character of myth, but as a living ideal- a compass for navigating the challenges of modem life with grace, courage, and resilience.

May this book serve as a gentle reminder that the path to divine is a journey of the heart, and that with Hanuman as our guide, we are never truly alone.

Nitish Mishra
Minister
Dept. of Industries
Govt. of Bihar

CONTENTS

Saga of Hanumān: A Universally Venerated Deity.

<u>INTRODUCTION</u>

When I undertook the exercise of compiling this book, its basic purpose was to translate into English in a lucid way Hanumān Chālīsā, Bajrang Bāṇ, etc. so that they become readily accessible to one and all. While Hanumānji is well known to everybody who has anything to do with Indian culture, as I began to collect information for this project, **I felt there were some facets of Hanumānji's persona which were not widely appreciated. I thought I should highlight them right in the beginning and hence this introduction.**

First, Hanumān was no doubt born to a monkey mother. But he totally transcended his monkeyhood. The refrain in Hanumānaṣṭaka goes as:

"को नहिं जानत है जग में
कपि संकटमोचन नाम तिहारो

"Who is not aware,
Your monikar is nothing but,
A refuge in difficult times"

Here the word कपि is often translated as "Oh! Great Monkey!"
We have in this text scrupulously avoided doing so.

This is because Hanumānji was a deity, and a great one at that; if he had merely the appearance of a monkey that can in no way become the subject of his appellation. Hanumānji was very much a divine being.

This is seen from numerous temples dedicated to him alone as well as his inclusion along with other deities in various shrines. We have therefore always alluded to Hanumānji by using terms such as Lord, Swami, Mahatma as befitting his sublimity.

Secondly, Hanumānji is usually looked upon solely within the context of Rāmāyana. While he was no doubt the greatest devotee of Lord Rāma and while he played a stellar role in latter's epic war with Rāvana, Hanumānji also had a close linkage with Śivaji; in fact, he and Ganeshji have a similar kind of relationship with the latter. **Hanumān is described as 'शंकर सुवन' or embodiment of Shankarji both in Hanumān Chālīsā and Bajrang Bāṇ.** This is because Bhagwan Shankar through Lord Kesari (Hanumanji's earthly father) had put a part of his splendour into the womb of Anjani (the mother of Hanumanji). This is precisely how Ganeshji too had emerged. As a result both get the appellation 'शंकर सुवन'.

It is due to the close linkage between Hanumānji and Śivaji that there are many temples where only the icon of Śivaji and an image of Hanumānji are worshipped. The reason why there are so many statues, carvings of Hanumānji in south-east Asia which were constructed prior to the 14th century probably lies in his linkage with Śivaji. This part of the world was then dominated by Cholas from Southern India who were staunch Śaivites. Some of the famous temples of Śivaji in South India were built by them. The word "Chola" which usually refers to this dynasty can can also mean, significantly enough, a paste made of sindoor, camphor oil, etc., used for anointing deities especially Hanumān.

In Indian iconography one clearly sees the close linkage between Śivaji and Hanumānji. To give one instance: in Kerala in Chenkal there is a famous Śiva–Parvati temple where the Śivaji's icon is a more than 110 feet in height which is reputedly highest in the world. Near the top of the icon we see the figure of Hanumanji in a flying posture. There is a famous temple of Hanumānji near the C.P., New Delhi. Next to it is an ancient Śiva temple which legend traces to the Mahābhārat era; significantly adjacent to it is a Ganesh temple. Thus Śivaji's temple is sandwiched between those of Hanumānji and Ganeshji – both 'शंकर सुवन'. Moreover, this Hanumān temple has a most unusual feature. **At the top of its spire is a lunar crescent in the same way as it appears on Śivaji's head. The reader will**

surely agree this is a pointer to the close bond between Śivaji and Hanumānji. (See the appended photograph)

Hanumanji therefore cannot be envisioned solely within the framework of Rāmāyana. His role extends far beyond it. We all know he protected Arjuna during the war with Kauravas by appearing on his chariot. (See the appended photograph, page 4)

The lunar crescent on the top of the spire of the Hanumān mandir, C.P., is clearly visible.

Finally, to say a few words about Hanumān Chālisā. During the course of writing this book I interacted with a number of people about this hymn. I found it was widely popular and many could recite it from memory easily and quote its stanzas. But I hardly came across anybody who could similarly recite verses from the Gita. Why was it so? I wondered.

The explanation which occurred to me was the following. Lord Krishna indeed promises bliss but that comes after a long haul only when the person has managed to reach the highest pinnacle of spirituality. **But in Hanumān Chālisā Hanumānji is invoked to provide instantaneous relief and succour to his devotee:** merely turn to Hanumānji with love and faith, and he is sure to ward off everything that is plaguing you, including even the ghosts and evil spirits. Citing here from Hanumān Chālisā

भूत पिशाच निकट नहिं आवै
महावीर जब नाम सुनावै

"Ghosts, goblins and evil souls
Dare not approach,
Where is heard
The (mere) recital of your (glorious) name,
Oh! Hanumānji, Oh! Hero"

[Verse No. 24]

Hanumānji thus stands by the devotee like a strong father and without any admonishing relieves him of his distress and overcomes his worries. This is why in Hanumānaṣṭaka Hanumānji is repeatedly hailed as:

"को नहिं जानत है जग में कपि संकटमोचन नाम तिहारो"

While Lord Krishna of the Gita is also the guardian of all he offers no instant remedy to devotee's ills. Instead he asks him to nurture detachment and to rise above worldly matters. Moreover, the language of Hanumān Chālisā is Avadhi which is a local tongue in U.P.

Mighty Hanumānji perched majestically on Arjuna's victorious chariot.

while its words are simple and folkish. The same cannot be said about the Gita.

In view of this is it any wonder Hanumān Chālisā has proved immensely popular to this day across all ages. It is looked upon as a source of solace by people of all ages. Moreover, it represents for them the very essence of Hinduism

In the end we can do no better than intone the following chaupai from Hanumān Chālisā:

सब सुख लहै तुम्हारी सरना
तुम रक्षक काहू को डरना

"Why be fearful of anything,
With you, oh! Hanumānji,
Standing by as the guardian;
By his grace,
All the pleasures and happiness
(of the world),
Will surely be yours."

(No. 22)

Finally I will like to share with the readers my personal experience while putting together the material for this book. During the course of its writing I found I was slowly but inevitably turning into a devotee of Hanumānji. I found he was gradually liberating me from my fears and irrational thoughts. These are the ghosts and demons which he drives away as mentioned in verse no. 24 of Hanumān Chālisā cited earlier.

Let us therefore bow before Hanumānji and earnestly seek his succour lovingly and full of faith. He is the Father and Guardian of all. He drives away all fears, whether of ghosts or calamities or death.

AUTHOR'S PREFACE

Hanumānji - A Paramount Deity, possessed of multi-faceted splendour

When one looks at the pantheon of Hindu deities one is truly amazed. What a scene it presents, and a fantastic one at that. There are so many and so many of them, some big, some small, some major, some minor. While each deity has its pre-assigned role to play, they often quarrel and struggle for supremacy. However, along with its plurality of deities, Hinduism also holds that there is a Supreme Being who towers above all. Usually this place of honour is given to Lord Vishnu of whom Rāma and Krishna are the main incarnations around whom are woven the great epics of the Rāmāyana and the Māhabhārata.

Apart from the Supreme Being there are two or three major deities of Hinduism such as Śankarji or Mahadevji, Brahmaji, the creator of the universe and various manifestations of the spouse of Śivaji like Durgaji, Kaliji, etc.

It may be wondered where in such a large gathering of gods and goddesses Hanumānji would figure. As we all know he is portrayed as a humble follower of Lord Rāma and the primary purpose of his life was to carry out the missions of Lord Rāma and Sitāji. By all accounts he may appear prima facie as a subordinate deity in the hierarchy of celestial beings. But this would be a grossly incorrect portrayal of Hanumānji.

It needs to be emphasized that a very large number of temples are dedicated exclusively to Hanumānji. One can find his temple in every nook and corner in any part of India. **Incidentally, one of the oldest temples of Hanumānji, 'Shri Panchmukhi Hanumān Temple', is situated in Karachi, Pakistan, and is said to be no less than 1500 years old.** People everywhere, young and old, pray to him for strength and resilience during difficult times. They recite Hanumān Chālisā when faced with a major crisis, and seek Hanumānji's blessings to get over it.

At such times surprisingly they do not turn to Vishnuji or Lord Rāma or Lord Krishna but to Hanumānji, though he is certainly not of their status. The Hanumān temple on Janpath, New Delhi, always attracts a large number of worshippers including prominent politicians. But why talk about only the Hanumān temple on Janapath. Hanumān temples everywhere, though many of them are linked by roads in poor condition, are usually thronged with devotees. People pray to him not mainly for wealth and fame as they do in case of other deities, but for removing obstacles from their life and warding off evil influences.

To give an instance of how popular is the worship of Hanumānji: Out of seven days in the week each one is closely associated with some deity. For instance, Monday is generally regarded as especially suitable for the worship of Mahadevji. But Hanumānji has a unique distinction in that out of these seven days two days are reserved for him, namely, Tuesdays and Saturdays. On these two days there is a marked increase in the rush to Hanumānji temples.

It is in view of the widespread popularity of Hanumānji and the deep faith which people have in him that we have in this little tract given the original texts of four main devotional lyrics dedicated to him, namely, Hanumān Chālisā, Bajrang Bāṇ, Hanumān Aṣṭaka and Hanumān Arti along with their transliteration and English translation. We hope this will make these hymns easily understandable to foreigners and members of the Indian diaspora who are not familiar with the Devanāgari script. Hanumān Chālisā is the most well known and widely recited lyric among them.

Praying to Hanumānji is regarded as a sure pathway to reaching the highest abode after death. The Hanumān Aarti in its last stanza says that a person who intones it regularly is bound to reach the supreme abode of Vishnuji or Vaikuntha, and thus escape the painful cycle of birth and death. This verse goes as:

"जो हनुमानजी की आरती गावै

बसि बैकुण्ठ परम पद पावै"

"Jo Hanumānji kī Ārtī Gave,
Basi Vaikuntha parama
Pada Pāve"

One who recites the Arti of Hanumānji,
(Full of faith),
Attains Vaikunth, the Supreme Abode."

The Gita explains how Vaikuntha is a place where liberated souls reside. It declares:

न तद्भासयते सूर्यो न शशाङ्को न पावकः ।
यद्गत्वा न निवर्तन्ते तद्धाम परमं मम ।।   (15/6)

na tadbhāsayate sūryo
na śaśānko na pāvakaḥ
Yad gatvà na nivartante
taddhāma paramaṁ mama   (15/6)

That is the Supreme Abode of mine (of Lord Krishna),
Neither the sun, nor the moon nor fire,
Illuminate it;
Those who reach it,
Do not return (to this world)"
(Escaping thus the cycle of birth and death)"   [Gita 15.6][1]

But the reader may legitimately wonder here as to what makes Hanumānji such a widely venerated deity. His lineage is not particularly impressive as he belongs to the lowly monkey clan. He is not invested with any outstanding physical beauty or glamour. Moreover, he does not possess weapons of magical power like Krishna's Sudarshan Chakra. But despite all these shortcomings, if one may say so, **he occupies the top rung**

---

[1] Transliterations in this text of Sanskrit verses are from the "Bhagavad Gita" by S. Radhakrishnan.

among the deities being worshipped in India. How has this come about?

<u>Hanumānji - The Real Protagonist of the Rāmāyana</u>

To find an answer to this seeming paradox one has only to look at Hanumānji's life and personality. **Hanumānji is the real hero of Rāmāyana.** Some may disagree with this and say that the real hero is Bhagawan Rāma followed by Sitāji and Laxman. **But had Hanumānji been not there what would have happened?** Without Hanumānji is it conceivable Lord Rāma would have succeeded in vanquishing and destroying the demons led by Rāvana? Without Hanumānji it is no exaggeration to say there would have been no Rāmāyana.

It was he who leaped across the wide ocean to find out the whereabouts of Sitāji about whom nothing was definitely known until then. It was he who brought the Sanjeevani plant from distant Himālayās to Lankā to save the life of Lakshmanji which was slowly ebbing away. It is only due to the unparalleled courage and the indomitable will of Hanumānji to overcome any challenge that Lord Rāma emerged victorious in his vicious battle with Rāvana and his demonic army with all their magical wiles and evil stratagems.

While there are many, many religious texts, among them Rāmāyana undoubtedly occupies an iconic place. There is hardly an Indian who is not acquainted with Rāmāyana and who is not familiar with its various episodes.

As a result Hanumānji's exploits and feats of valour have become common knowledge. This cannot be said about wicked demons killed by Śankarji or Kaliji. **In view of all this adoration of Hanumānji and praying to him for strength and courage comes naturally to most people. This is why he is adored universally.**

<u>**Portrayal of Hanumānji**</u>

How does one characterise Hanumānji? Obviously his foremost quality was total and absolute devotion to Lord Rāma. There was nothing in his life except serving Him; his heart was full of faith in Lord Rāma as well as overflowing with love of him.

Hanumānji epitomised the ideal devotee as described in the Gita. Lord Krishna says one should do everything in the name of God, surrender oneself totally to Him and be totally free of any feeling of ego. We quote here a relevant stanza from the Gita.

मन्मना भव मद्भक्तो मद्याजी मां नमस्कुरु।
मामेवैष्यसि युक्त्वैवमात्मानं मत्परायणः।।   (9/34)

manmanā bhava madbhakto
madyājī māṁ namaskuru
māmevaiṣyasi yuktvaivam atmānaṁ matparāyaṇaḥ (9.34)

"Let your mind be full of Me (Supreme Being);
Be my devotee, worship Me;
Pay obeisance to Me;
Look upon Me as the Supreme;
In this way,
You will then attain Me,
Being wholly self-restrained"   [Gita 9.34]

Hanumānji evidently was a personification of such an ideal devotee. This is why on one occasion when he had ripped apart his heart what was seen there were only Lord Rāma and Sitāji. **It is said that when one reaches the ultimate Nirvana man becomes God. This is what had happened in case of Hanumānji. [See the enclosed picture on the next page.]**

He possessed enormous strength. We are all familiar with the figure of Hanumānji carrying a huge chunk of a mountain on which was the Sanjeevani plant all the way from the Himālayās for saving the life of Lakshmanji. He fought with horrible demons with bare hands and easily squashed them into pulp. He alone went to the nether world and extricated Lord Rāma and Lakshmanji from the clutches of AhiRāvan and his wicked tribe.

Hanumānji proudly displaying Rāma, Sitā and Laxmanji ensconed within his heart.

This is why in the Hanumān Aṣṭaka he is described as 'one who saves the devotee from every danger' and this is the refrain of its eight verses which goes as:

"को नहिं जानत है जग में, कपि सिंकटमोचन नाम तिहारो"

*"Ko Nahin Jānata Hain Jaga men kapi,
Sankata Mochana Nama Tiharo"*

"Who is not aware in this world, Oh! Swami,
Your epithet is nothing else than,
One who provides refuge in calamity"

While possessed of such magnificent virtues, there was a certain degree of simplicity and child-like innocence about Hanumānji. In the Ashokvan after battling and crushing into dust the horrible demons there he climbed one of its trees, and calmly started plucking the fruits thereof. He was thus behaving exactly like any other monkey grabbing fruits from trees.

It is this simplicity of Hanumānji which makes an ordinary devotee experience a certain kinship for him. Such a sense of kinship for Hanumānji coupled with his absolute faith in Lord Rāma and his stupendous and incomparable strength have made Hanumānji the object of deepest reverence of one and all.

Hanumānji - A Great Diplomat

Another distinguishing trait of Hanumānji was his tactfulness. In fact he had great diplomatic skills. **Our foreign minister S Jaishankar has described Hanumānji as one of the greatest diplomats known to India. Why is it so?**

Hanumānji's ability to gain confidence of strangers and to talk with them in an appropriate manner as befits the situation comes out vividly during his first encounter with Sitāji. Let us try to put ourselves in that scenario.

Sitāji was cut off for a long time from Lord Rāma after being abducted by demon Rāvana. She had no news of her beloved husband. She was surrounded by horrible demonesses who were all the time trying to break her down. They were desperate to convince her that there was no possibility that a mere mortal like Rāma, and a weak one at that, could possibly cross the huge ocean and challenge a mighty demon like Rāvana. To make things worse for her the demon king Rāvana used to visit her from time to time, and try to induce her to marry him, emphasising that Lord Rāma had abandoned her, and that as his beloved queen she would enjoy unimaginable luxuries and pleasures. All this was most detestful and revolting to Sitāji. But she had to put up with such odious words silently unable to retaliate in any way. She would suffer and suffer experiencing extreme anguish.

As the days passed she had become increasingly despondent and morose. She was seriously contemplating committing suicide, and was wondering as she sat below the Ashok tree as to the best way of ending her life. It was at this juncture that Hanumānji had come to the Ashokvan and found her. How did he go about introducing himself?

Had Hanumānji approached her in his usual form with his huge body carrying a threatening mace no doubt Sitāji would have been frightened out of her wits. She would have believed that Hanumānji was none but a demon sent by Rāvana to further molest and torment her. But the arch diplomat that he was Hanumānji does nothing of this kind. He assumes a very tiny shape and initially drops a memento given by Lord Rāma to him which was his signet ring. It falls next to where Sitāji was sitting bemoaning her cruel fate and wailing; Hanumānji was then perched on the Ashoka tree just above her.

Looking at the ring which had apparently fallen from the sky Sitāji became overjoyed. Hanumānji then in a soft voice started extolling the various sterling qualities of Lord Rāma. Sitāji gradually got absorbed in listening to the narrative of Hanumānji, and forgot her own woes and miseries. When Hanumānji felt that Sitāji was sufficiently composed that he came down from the tree, and introduced himself to her as an emissary of Lord Rāma.

So impressive and credible was the presentation of various qualities of Lord Rāma made by Hanumānji and so sincere was his mode of conduct that Sitāji had little difficulty in at once accepting him as Lord Rāma's emissary and his great devotee.

Thus developed a bond of great respect and affection between Sitāji and Hanumānji which lasted forever and ever. Sitāji blessed Hanumānji with choicest boons as a result of which when demons had set fire to his tail he was not in the least hurt.

There are many other episodes in Rāmāyana where one clearly observes Hanumānji's tactfulness. We give here some instances of the same.

How Hanumānji befriended strangers:

During the epochal war with Rāvana Lakshmanji was mortally wounded by a potent missile hurled by his son Indrajeet. He had become unconscious and his life was slowly slipping away. It was clear to everybody that he did not have long to live. Even Lord Rāma had lost his courage, and was profusely shedding tears with Lakshmanji's head on his lap. At that time it was Hanumānji who rose to the occasion and found a way out of this great catastrophe.

He jumped over the ramparts of Lankā and boldly entered it; he then took hold of the physician of Rāvana who was known for his great diagnostic skills. The physician naturally was aghast to find that he was abducted in this manner and was taken to the enemy camp. He initially totally refused to minister to Lakshmanji, but Hanumānji did not lose his cool. He spoke with him in a most humble way, and persuaded him to take care of the mortally wounded Lakshmanji. How did he do so?

Hanumānji emphasised that as a physician it was incumbent upon him to treat all patients who were brought to him, and it was not for him to bother whether a particular person was his friend or foe. So persuasive was Hanumānji that the physician agreed to diagnose Lakshmanji's injury and suggested that he could be saved only if the Sanjeevani plant could be brought all the way from distant Himālayās, and that too within the next twenty-four hours.

We all know what happened subsequently. Hanumānji in a giant leap managed to reach the Himālayās, and carried back with him a huge chunk of that mountain on which fluttered the Sanjeevani plant. With its juice Lakshmanji was revived and he stood up to challenge Indrajit whom he vanquished after a fierce fight.

But all this would have been impossible had Hanumānji not brought the royal physician of Rāvana to cater to Lakshmanji as he faced the gravest danger of his life. It is noteworthy that Hanumānji never threatened Rāvana's

physician in any way, and only through tactfulness and courtesy he secured his cooperation. This should be a lesson for all of us.

We can give many examples which vividly illustrate Hanumānji's ability to conduct himself in the most appropriate manner as the situation demanded.

Let us review the events which took place when Hanumānji entered Lankā for the first time. He was moving around and everywhere he saw demons and their mansions. He found that the demons as per their nature were engaged in barbaric activities and everywhere there were scenes which were revolting and horrifying.

However, Hanumānji came across a house from which holy sounds like "Om" were emerging. He saw near that residence signs of sacred rituals being performed. Hanumānji started wondering how could in a demonic city such a house could exist and who would be its occupant.

As he was thus pondering a figure emerged from that residence. Hanumānji wanted to find out who that person was, but he did not do so in his original monkey form. He transformed himself into a Brahmin and went near that individual, and then introducing himself accordingly asked as to who he was.

He turned out to be none other than Vibhishan, a great devotee of Lord Rāma, whose heart was all the time yearning to be with the Lord. Gradually Hanumānji came to know that the person who was talking to him was none other than Rāvana's younger brother, but who happened to be totally different from him and whose total loyalty was to Lord Rāma.

Hanumānji was naturally most gratified, and he decided that it was an opportune time to introduce himself in a truthful way to Vibhishan. He did so. We all know that Vibhishan was to subsequently prove a great ally and a loyal follower of Lord

Rāma. He was invaluable to him while the war was going on with Rāvana.

But all this proved possible only because Hanumānji had the courage to approach politely a stranger in a city inhabited by wicked demons, and to identify somebody who was wholly committed to the path of Dharma and who sought nothing but Lord Rāma's grace.

We will cite another instance where again Hanumānji displayed great sagacity and circumspection. Sugreeva, the younger brother of Bāli, was expelled by the latter from Kinshāsā, their capital city. One day Sugreeva was sitting on a hill along with Hanumānji and other monkeys. They saw two strangers armed with bows majestic in appearance approaching them. As a result Sugreeva became extremely apprehensive as Bāli had threatened to get him killed. He thought the strangers were somebody sent by Bāli to slay him.

But he decides to send Hanumānji to ascertain who they were. Hanumānji then assumes a human shape and approaches them. Gradually Hanumānji came to know that they were Lord Rāma and his brother Lakshman who were wandering here and there engaged in a desperate search of Sitāji. Hanumānji felt that here was an opportunity for Sugreeva to recover his kingdom and at the same time to be of great great service to Lord Rāma.

He advises Sugreeva to meet Lord Rāma and Laxmanji who then does so, and thus was born a deep friendship between them which was to last forever. Sugreeva fought loyally by the side of Lord Rāma in the great war with Rāvana, and gave him total and unstinted support. **Here again while the end was most felicitous it proved possible only because Hanumānji could gain the confidence of Lord Rāma and Laxmanji who were then strangers to him and befriend them.**

Hanumānji's total self-control and equanimity:

We now turn to another episode. It relates to the period when Hanumānji was crossing the ocean to reach Lankā. Suddenly he found that his way was being blocked by a demoness called Sursā. She was standing in his path with her mouth wide open. When Hanumānji saw her he magnified his own body to twice the dimension of that demoness's mouth. Thereupon the demoness also expanded her mouth to twice of that of Hanumānji's body. Hanumānji again does the same thing. This went on for some time with both Hanumānji and Sursā magnifying and enlarging themselves more and more.

Hanumānji then understood the futility of engaging in this exercise. He knew his purpose was not to kill Sursā or to get involved in unnecessary altercations with strangers, but to reach Lankā at the earliest. He therefore assumes a tiny form, enters the mouth of Sursā, and quickly passes out through her other end. Sursā also realized that Hanumānji was truly an exceptional personality and commended him.

This story shows that Hanumānji knew when to stop fighting and when to accept even a lowly posture in order to gain one's ends. Hanumānji was always most self-restrained and had full control over himself, his emotions, and his senses. He invariably displayed extreme coolness of temperament and equability. We see all these great qualities of Hanumānji during his first encounter with Rāvana in Lankā. Let us take our mind to that scenario.

Hanumānji had entered Lankā, an impregnable city as it was then known to be, and managed to wreak much damage there. He had killed a number of demons and even vanquished and crushed to death a son of Rāvana, one Akshaya Kumar, who was himself a redoubtable warrior. Indrajeet, the eldest son of Rāvana, had then come to confront Hanumānji. After a fierce fight Indrajeet hurled Bramhastra at Hanumānji. Though the latter was in no way affected by it he allowed himself to be bound and fettered to show respect to that astra which belonged to Brahma.

In that state he was taken to the assembly hall of Rāvana who was sitting in all splendour along with his deputies and others. Hanumānji was being taunted and humiliated as he was taken to the presence of great Rāvana, who in turn spoke with him in a jeering tone abusing Hanumānji and not showing him the least courtesy.

But Hanumānji was not in the least ruffled by all this. He did not lose his composure. There was not a trace of anger in him. He did not threaten Rāvana with reprisals or of severe retribution being brought down upon him. He merely asked him to return Sitāji to Lord Rāma, and accept him as the Ruler of the Universe. He assures Rāvana that if he did so he will continue to enjoy the rulership of Lankā, and Lord Rāma would treat him with utmost graciousness.

Of course Ravana was in no mood to listen to all this. He treated Hanumānji with the greatest disdain and discourtesy possible. Hanumānji still did not get discomfited. He asked Rāvana or rather entreated him to move away from the path of Adharma, to give up his ego and arrogance, and to follow the teachings of Dharma. He warned him that if Rāvana did not do so his whole clan would meet a terrible end. Following stanza from Sunderkand will illustrate how earnestly and humbly Hanumānji was urging Rāvana to follow the path of Dharma.

"बिनती करउँ जोरि कर रावन। सुनहु मान तजि मोर सिखावन॥
देखहु तुम्ह निज कुलहि बिचारी। भ्रम तजि भजहु भगत भय हारी॥"

"Binantī Karau Jori Kara Rāvana,
Sunahu, Māna Taji Mora Sikhāvan,
Dekhahu Tumha Nija Kulahi Bichari,
Bhrama Taji Bhajahu Bhagat Bhaya Harī."

Oh! Rāvana!
With folded hands (in supplication),
I entreat you;
Please listen to my counsel,
Giving up your ego,
Think about your clan,
And ponder over (their) (future);
Get rid of your delusion,
Turn to adoration,
Of the Lord,
Dispeller of the fear of devotees;"

But what is noteworthy here in no way Hanumānji was threatening or abusive towards Rāvana, though the latter had spared no efforts to heap every possible insult on him. **He thus gave an ideal example of how a man should always maintain his equanimity, no matter what his sufferings or torments.** Here one is reminded of the following stanza from the Gita.

समः शत्रौ च मित्रे च तथा मानापमानयोः।
शीतोष्णसुखदुःखेषु समः सङ्गविवर्जितः॥   (12/18)

samah śatrau ca mitre ca
tathā mānāpamānayoh
śītoṣṇasukhadukhkheṣu
samah saṅgavivarjitah   (12/18)

"One who is the same towards foes and friends,
Who remains the same,
Be it praise or abuse,
Whom heat or cold, happiness or sorrow,
Do not affect,
One who is devoid of attachment."   [12.18]

In fact, one feels that Hanumānji was a personification of whatever is laid down in the Gita. Hanumānji also had the greatest of humility. Though he had done magnificent deeds and though his accomplishments were extraordinary, he did not have the slightest pride. He did everything in the name of

Lord Rāma, and took no credit for his achievements. He was truly a Karma Yogi par excellence.

<u>Hanumānji's extraordinary humility:</u>

This is best seen from the following: Hanumānji had returned from Lankā; he had then met Sitāji, brought a memento from her for presenting it to Lord Rāma, and given her the courage to withstand her ordeal for a few more days till Lord Rāma came to rescue her.

She was in fact on the verge of committing suicide when Hanumānji had met her. But thanks to Hanumānji's assurance she had agreed not to take such a desperate step, and to await the arrival of her beloved husband. Earlier after crossing the ocean and entering Lankā, Hanumānji had crushed to death many demons including the sons of Rāvana and openly defied him, setting fire to a large part of his impregnable, golden city.

When Hanumānji was pressed by Lord Rāma to narrate what he had done in Lankā he spoke in a very modest way as if his achievements were next to nothing. Here we quote a stanza from Sundarkand which goes as follows:

"साखामृग कै बड़ि मनुसाई। साखा तें साखा पर जाई॥
नाघि सिंधु हाटकपुर जारा। निसिचर गन बिधि बिपिन उजारा॥"

"Sākhāmṛga kai Badi Manusāī,
Sākhā te Sākhā para Jāī,
Nāghi Sindhu Hātankpura Jārā,
Nisichara Gana Bidhi Bipin Ujārā"

"No great deal is it for a monkey,
To hop from a bough to bough;
Crossing the ocean,
I burnt the golden city (Lankā);
I killed some demons,
And laid waste to the grove (Ashokavara)."

This is an ideal example of how a person should always remain modest no matter what his attainments are.

Hanumānji - The Mahatma

We are now in a position to sketch the wonderful personality of Hanumānji: indeed what a fantastic and unbelievable personality it truly turns out to be! Hanumānji is totally free of any passion, any vicious thought, any kind of lust, anything that can taint the human mind. **He is as pure as a shining crystal, and can very much be described as a great, great saint. This is why he is addressed as 'Mahatma'.**

But along with being pure-hearted and saintly, he was totally fearless. He did not ever have the slightest hesitation in confronting the biggest and most vicious demons, never doubting for a minute that he would be able to vanquish them. He all by himself went to the netherworld where the vicious AhiRāvana along with his cohorts had established his wicked reign. He succeeded in freeing Lord Rāma and Lakshmanji from the clutches of that cruel demon and put to death all his evil companions. No danger, no threat, ever meant anything to Hanumānji. This is why it is said in Hanumān Aṣṭaka that by praying to Hanumānji all the evils are warded off from the devotee.

As far as Hanumānji's strength is concerned it beggars description. We only have to imagine how he carried single-handedly a chunk of the giant Himālayās to get some idea of his colossal power. One indeed wonders whether anybody else could have remotely equalled Hanumānji in his physical capabilities.

But along with all these qualities he was the most tactful of persons, very gentle and very modest. He could easily befriend strangers, win their confidence and count on their help. This is clearly seen from the episode relating to Rāvana's physician narrated earlier. Hanumānji had forcibly brought him to Lord Rāma's camp. But still he could induce him to minister to the mortally-wounded Laxmanji in a most courteous way.

Hanumānji - The Confluence of Gyana (Knowledge), Bhakti (devotion) and Nishkam Karma (detached action)

Hanumānji sought nothing for himself. His life was devoted to the service of Lord Rāma, to the service of Dharma. He was a true Gyana Yogi, a true Karma Yogi, a true Bhakta.

Sundarkand in its very beginning described Hanumānji as an ocean of knowledge and of sterling virtues. This verse goes as follows:

अतुलितबलधामं हेमशैलाभदेहं दनुजवनकृशानुं
ज्ञानिनामग्रगण्यम्।
सकलगुणनिधानं वानराणामधीशं रघुपतिप्रियभक्तं वातजातं
नमामि।।

Atulitbaladhāmam Hemshailābhdeham,
Danujavana Kṛshānum Gyanināmagraganyam,
Sakalgunnidhānam Vānarānāmadheesham,
Raghupatipriyabhaktam Vatajatam Namami"

"I pay my obeisance to the son of the wind-god (Hanumānji),
The beloved devotee of Bhagwan Rāma,
The Lord of the monkeys,
Foremost among the wise,
Possessed of incomparable strength,
With a body having lustre like the mountain of gold (Sumeru),
Repository of all sterling virtues,
Setting fire to a multitude of demons,
As if to a forest"

So absolute and and all-encompassing was Hanumānji's faith in Lord Rāma that he could wage vicious battles with utmost calmness without any passion. He thus personified Gita's teachings as given in the following two stanzas:

मयि सर्वाणि कर्माणि संन्यस्याध्यात्मचेतसा।
निराशीर्निर्ममो भूत्वा युध्यस्व विगतज्वरः ॥   (3/30)

mayi sarvāṇi karmāṇi,
Saṁnyasyādhyātma-cetasā !
nirāśīrnirmamo bhūtvā,
yudhyasva vigatajvaraḥ   (3/30)

"Dedicating all your actions to Me (Supreme Lord),
With consciousness focused in (your) the divine soul;
Without any expectations,
Or a sense of ego,
Wage this battle,
Free of any passion."   [3.30]

तस्मात्सर्वेषु कालेषु मामनुस्मर युध्य च।
मय्यर्पितमनोबुद्धिर्मामेवैष्यस्यसंशय: ॥

tasmāt sarveṣu kāleṣu
māmanusmara yudhya ca
mayyarpitamanobuddhir
māmevaiṣyasyasaṁsayaḥ.

Therefore at all times,
Remembering Me (Lord Krishna) (only),
Fight (this war);
With your mind and body,
Attuned entirely to Me (the Lord);
Undoubtedly you will
Become one with Me (the Lord)."   [8.7]

Hanumānji thus exemplified the sublime message of these stanzas.

This is what an average individual should try to emulate in his daily life as far as possible. **Hanumānji thus becomes eminently suitable for supreme reverence by all of us.**

But what perhaps distinguishes Hanumānji from other deities more than anything else is the following.

Hanumānji - The greatest of the great

Lord Rāma, as we all know, was no ordinary mortal. He was an incarnation of Vishnuji himself, the creator, sustainer and destroyer of the world. There was no entity in this world or in the heaven who could even remotely approach Lord Rāma. It is said that even Yama, the god of death whom all feared, trembled before Lord Rāma, and that all the elements took orders from him.

But it was Lord Rāma who was protected from grave dangers not once but many times by Hanumānji as is vividly brought out in Rāmāyana. One can easily thus envisage Hanumānji's all-surpassing aura and his fantastic powers if he could give succour to a Being like Lord Rāma who was the creator of the universe itself. Hanumānji is also described as the guardian of Lord Rāma's Darbar or sacred assembly. If one is to find salvation or reach Lord Rāma, then the way to him passes through the grace of Hanumānji.

While possessed of all such miraculous qualities, traits and virtues, Hanumānji remained extremely modest with a childlike innocent face. He never appears remote from ordinary human beings, and is someone whom one feels one can trust and regard as one's companion.

This is why during celebration of Rāma lilā it is the actor playing the role of Hanumānji who usually attracts maximum attention. Children throng around him to shake his hands and to be photographed with him so impressed are they by Hanumānji's wondrous feats.

A young boy no more than 11 or 12 years old who regularly recites Hanumān Chālisā told the author once that when he remembers Hanumānji a surge of energy and confidence passes through his body. He also said this did not happen when he takes the name of any other god or goddess.

There is another factor which has fostered Hanumānji's popularity and made him a household deity. It is nothing but his herculean strength. As a result he is the favourite idol of wrestlers and body-builders. It is before the image of Hanumānji that wrestlers bow down prior to beginning their training and exercises.

Is it any wonder then in view of Hanumānji's extraordinary personality, his dazzling radiance and overarching power that he has become the object of veneration all over India. We find his temples small and big everywhere from north to south, from east to west. Some temples are no doubt grand but some are also very small where there is only a tiny image of Hanumānji. It makes no difference what the size of his image is like. It is the deep faith of the devotees and their trust in his miraculous powers to help them in distress which drives them towards worshipping him with greatest fervour.

Talking about the temples of Hanumānji we might here observe an unusual feature associated with them. There are many many temples where Hanumānji alone is the deity to be worshipped. Of course there are numerous temples of Lord Rāma where with him are worshipped Sitāji, Lakshmanji, Hanumānji, etc. But we hardly come across a temple where there is only Sitāji to be worshipped or only Lakshmanji; in fact with the exception of a newly-established temple in Sitāmadhi in the Mithilānchal region of Bihār which is dedicated to Sitāji, it would be difficult to identify a temple in India where Sitāji is the principal deity. There is one major temple in Nepal too where Sitāji is mainly worshipped. But these are exceptions. As regards Laxmanji and other iconic figures of Ramāyana no temples are known to be there exclusively for their worship.

But Hanumānji, on the other hand, falls into an altogether different category. Like Śivaji or Kālji there are innumerable temples where Hanumānji is the sole deity; in various temples one finds idols or carvings of Hanumānji along with those of other gods and goddesses. Moreover, there are several temples dedicated exclusively to adoration of only Śivaji and Hanumānji while in some shrines sculptures of Hanumānji and Ganeshji are prominently displayed on the entrance of the sanctum sanctorum. All this clearly brings out the exalted status of Hanumānji in the Hindu pantheon. **By putting Hanumānji on the same pedestal as Śivaji and Ganeshji both pre-eminent deities, it is unmistakably conveyed that Hanumānji belongs to the highest echelon of deities.**

Hanumānji is also distinguished by his distinctive iconography. He is represented in widely different ways, sometimes in a threatening warrior pose, somewhere else as bearing on one hand a huge mountain, elsewhere as having more than one face, and so on. This tract is illustrated with pictures of Hanumānji in widely differing modes of depiction. (See the enclosed picture of Hanumānji in a meditative pose on the next page no.27) To project him as the greatest of Bhaktās (devotees), he is famously shown in a standing posture with his chest ripped apart where one observes only Lord Rāma, Sitāji and Laxmanji. (See page no.11)

Another noteworthy and rather unique feature of Hanumānji's iconography lies in his towering images. Idols of Hanumānji exceeding hundred feet in height and visible from a great distance are found in all parts of India which points to his pan-Indian status. Images of gods and goddesses usually resemble human beings, but an exception has been probably made about Hanumānji to emphasize his incomparable physical strength and power. [See the attached photograph on page 28]

A most unusual of Hanumānji's iconography is found in his temples called Shri Patāli (subterranean) Hanumān temples found all over India in places like Gwalior, Mumbai, Omkareshwar, etc., attracting a large number of devotees. In these temples there is a portrayal of battles fought by Hanumānji in the netherworld and especially his vanquishing of AhiRāvana and his demonic cohorts. In the Omkareshwar Patāli Hanumān mandir, there is a twenty-foot long image of Hanumān in a sleeping posture which lies about seven feet under the earth[2]; below the body of Hanumān are displayed the cowering figures of AhiRāvana and the presiding deity of the netherworld to whom AhiRāvana wanted to make the sacrificial offering of Lord Rāma and Laxmanji.

Moreover, it also noteworthy this shrine of Hanumān forms a part of major temple of Śivaji in Omkareswar where was found one of the twelve Jyotir lingas. This emphasizes the symbiotic relationship between Śivaji and Hanumānji to which we have repeatedly referred in this tract.

But it need not be thought that the worship of Hanumānji is confined only to the Indian sub-continent. **This cult is well-established in South-East Asia and that too from ancient times.** In the Angkor Wat temple complex built as early as the 12th century there are many, many impressive figures of Hanumānji. A famous mural there shows him leading a monkey army against Rāvana's demon forces. **In Sri Lanka there are several major pilgrimage sites centred on Hanumānji. These**

Hanumānji in a meditative posture.

include the site of his giant footprint indicating the place where he had landed after having crossed the sea. [See the enclosed picture on page 30.] Similarly, there are many shrines

---

[2] As per the legend Hanumānji rested in this place after slaying AhiRāvana and his evil forces.

dedicated to him in Malaysia, Cambodia and Indonesia where one also comes across several statues and depictions of Hanumānji which belong to 10th to 14th century. [See the enclosed pictures, page no. 31.]

In recent years India is following a "Far East" policy which calls for specially fostering links with this region. But as the murals, statues and temples of Hanumānji scattered over countries of S.E. Asia testify India's religio-cultural ties with this part of the world originate from far earlier times. In fact, they date back to 10th century A.D., when Cholās of Tāmil Nādu established an extensive maritime empire which encompassed large regions of S.E. Asia. The Cholās were ardent Śaivites and enthusiastic temple builders. There are giant ancient temples of Śiva in these countries which is the legacy of the Chola rule. As per Śaivism Hanumān is the eleventh incarnation of Rudra. It is no surprise therefore that all over

Towerubg figure of Hanumānji in the Paritalā Anjaneyā temple in Andhra Pradesh, around 135 feet in height.

South-East Asia one comes across temples, statues and carvings of Hanumān. **All this shows he was widely worshipped from Sri Lanka to Bali since ancient times. Thus we have with every justification described Hanumān as a 'Universally Venerated Deity' in the title to this tract.**

Hanumān Chalisā: Its special features

In view of the sublimity of Hanumānji and his divine personality many many lyrics have been composed in his adoration. Perhaps the foremost among them would be Hanumān Chālisā. It is a rhapsody which extols Hanumānji and glorifies his magnificent feats. It is a highly emotive and effusive text which touches one's heart.

Hanumān Chālisā is written in Awadhi by Tulsidāsji in simple words. They are easy to remember and recite. The verses are rhythmic and lyrical. They are two-line couplets with each line consisting of only 4/5 words. Moreover, the endings of both the lines in each couplet are invariably similar; all this greatly enhances their melody and poetic rhythm. Its recital is a source of great joy and inspiration.

This is the reason why Hanumān Chālisā is intoned by many many people, young and old, every day. People especially turn to it when they are in distress and through it they try to invoke Hanumānji's blessings to get over their difficulties, major or minor. This is why Hanumānji has been aptly described as 'Sankat Mochan' (one who invariably relieves the devotee of his problems, worries, etc.) repeatedly in Hanumānaṣṭka.

Hanumān Chālisa is recorded on YouTube by the renowned singer Anup Jalota, and has evoked a most enthusiastic response. This testifies to its vast popularity. But while being widely popular, it is also a much revered text. Many Hanumān devotees keep it with them as a means of protection[3].

Hanumān Chālisā has been passed from generation to generation in India, and there are many households where it is intoned only from memory without having a written text of it. This shows that it is an essential part of our culture and heritage. We all often talk of Indian culture but what do we precisely mean by it?

---

[3] T.O.I. dated 10.12.2025

Culture means not living merely in the present but learning from our glorious past and remembering what our forefathers and great forefathers had done in previous generations. We learn from them the difference between right and wrong, between morality and immorality, between dharma and adharma. **Awareness of one's culture widens one's horizon and one understands that there is far more to this world than meets the eye, and life is far more than merely chasing money by any means believing it to be the certain and only path to eternal happiness. How is this purpose served by the recital of Hanumān Chālisā?**

Giant footprint of Hanumānji, ŚriPada sacred rock formation in SriLanka.

Hanumān Chālisā is not merely a glorification of Hanumānji, the Venerable Swami. We also eulogize in it his sterling virtues like fearlessness, his unflinching commitment to duty, absolute devotion to Lord Rāma, etc. Worldly pleasures and wealth meant nothing to Hanumānji and what he sought was only the grace of Lord Rāma. **Hanumānji lived in a world which transcended our world of Maya, of sensual pleasures and pains, of**

dualities. Only a person who is highly spiritual can act in a totally detached and fearless manner as Hanumānji did throughout his life. Hanumān Chālisā therefore becomes a source of fortitude and mortality for the average individual as he goes through his life facing its myriad temptations. **One who recalls the feats of Hanumānji, one who draws inspiration from his conduct would not easily be swayed from the path of Dharma, from the path of righteousness by worldly temptations.**

Just as Hanumānji stands out by his unique personality in Rāmāyana so does Hanumān Chālisā in the genre of bhakti geets or devotional lyrics. Why do we say so?

Sant Tukaram's Abhangs or devotional verses, Meerabai's or Surdasji's portrayal of their deep piety and communion with Lord Krishna are justly famous and widely known. **But no one would recite their compositions, when one is facing an ordeal like an operation or undertaking a risky journey. At such a critical juncture it is to Hanumān Chālisā only they would turn to.**

Hanumānji's sculptures from the Chola period (9' th to 13' th centuries) belonging to South-East Āsia.

Perhaps what draws a clear line of demarcation between Hanumān Chālisā and compositions of medieval poet-saints is the fact that the former over the years has come to symbolize Hinduism, as well as Hindu culture and civilization. This is why it is a part of daily activities of R.S.S. cadres which they look upon as a source of "eternal knowledge".

Earlier in U.P. groups of Hindus had decided to recite Hanumān Chālisā in unison on streets in case members of another community were allowed to perform "Namaaz" in public areas. It is again only Hanumān Chālisā which is chanted when there are protests against human rights violations of Hindus in foreign countries.

There is another factor which probably greatly contributes to Hanumān Chālisā's popularity. This is nothing but its extreme brevity. Why is it so? The entire Hanumān Chālīsā can be unhurriedly sung or listened to in no more than seven/eight minutes. This much time can be spared easily by many even in today's busy times; and what a tremendous spiritual benefit it thus affords.

As they sing or listen to its lyrics, thrilling scenes from the Rāmāyana are evoked before their eyes in which Hanumānji played a stellar role. One is then reminded of his unwavering determination, absolute faith and total fearlessness. Listening to this lyric makes one reinvigorated and recharged. **Is it any wonder so many people have made it a part of their daily routine either in the morning or in the evening to sing or listen to this immortal hymn?**

When a person's horoscope shows the evil influence of some planet, the soothsayers usually recommend regular recital of Hanumān Chālisā by him/her to counteract it. This is why during the covid pandemic of 2020 onwards mass chanting of the Hanumān Chālisā was organized by the R.S.S. in different parts of the country through online platforms. Its daily recitation is supposed to be most beneficial; but if this is not possible, one should recite it at least on Tuesdays and Saturdays, the days which are specially associated with Hanumānji.

Truly Hanumān Chālisā is a living lyric. It lives in the hearts of people, young and old. To obliterate the fear of ghosts from the minds of young children, and to make them self-confident as well as optimistic mothers teach them its following verses:

भूत पिशाच निकट नहिं आवै।
महावीर जब नाम सुनावै ॥   (No. 23)

नासै रोग हरै सब पीरा ।
जपत निरंतर हनुमत बीरा ॥   (No. 24)

"Bhoot pishāch nikat nahin aawai
Mahaveer jab naam Sunawai"   (No. 23)

"Nāsai rog harai sab peerā
Japat Nirantar hanumat Veerā"   (No. 24)

"No ghost, goblin, evil spirit, etc.,
Dare approach,
Where the name of Hanumānji,
Of the great hero is heard"

[No. 23, Hanumān Chalisa]

Chant constantly the name of glorious Hanumānji,
Overcome will be all (your) afflictions,
All the difficulties will vanish."

[No 24, Hanumān Chalisa]

In the next part are the texts of four main devotional hymns, along with their transliteration and translation glorifying Hanumānji and they being: Hanumān Chālisā, Hanumān Aṣṭaka, Bajrang Baṇ, and Hanumān Ārti. All these lyrics especially the first three eloquently describe those events in Rāmāyana in which Hanumānji had played a momentous role like bringing the Sanjeevani plant from the Himālayās to the battlefield, entering the netherworld to rescue Shri Rāma and Lakshmanji from the evil clutches of AhiRāvana and his vicious demon companions, etc. By referring to these episodes the incredible exploits of

Hanumānji and his magnificent heroic deeds have been immortalized in them.

Regular recital of the above four hymns glorifying Hanumānji, constant meditation on him, and worshiping him with overwhelming faith and veneration, would prove highly beneficial to everybody. It would fulfil devotee's all worldly aspirations, afford him enjoyment of material pleasures within the framework of Dharma and, what is most important, pave his way to salvation. We have given below some citations from Hanuman Chalisa and other devotional hymns mentioned earlier which will bear this out.

"दुर्गम काज जगत के जेते
सुगम अनुग्रह तुम्हरे तेते"

*"Durgam kāj jagat ke jete
Sugam anugrah tumhare tete"*

"Whatever be your arduous worldly tasks,
Easy of fulfilment would they become,
If your (of Hanumānji's) grace is there"
[Verse no. 20, Hanumān Chālisā]

सब सुख लहै तुम्हारी सरना
तुम रक्षक काहू को डरना

*"Saba sukha lahai tumhārī Sarnā,
Tum rakshaka kahoo ko darnā"*

"All joys will automatically follow the one,
Whose refuge is yourself, Hanumānji;
Why should one fear anybody,
When you are the guardian"
[Verse 22, Hanumān Chālisā]

"संकट ते हनुमान छुड़ावै
मन क्रम वचन ध्यान जो लावै"

34

"Sankat te hunumān Chhuḍawai
Mana krama Bachana dhyān jo lāwai"

"One who meditates on you, Hanumānji,
Through thought, action and speech,
All the hurdles in his life,
Will disappear by your grace."

[Verse 26, Hanumān Chālisā]

"और मनोरथ जो कोई लावै
सोई अमित जीवन फल पावै"

"Aura manoratha jo koi lawai
Soi amita jeevana phala pawai"

Whatever be your hopes and aspirations,
(If Hanumānji has bestowed his grace on you),
The rewards of your life, shall be unbounded and beyond
description"

[Verse no. 28, Hanumān Chālisā,]

"तुम्हरे भजन राम को पावै,
जनम जनम के दुख बिसरावै"

"Tumhre bhajana Rāma ko pawai
Janama janama ke dukha visarāvai"
"Worshipping you, Hanumānji,
Is the certain pathway,
To being blessed by Bhagwan Rāma himself,
Leading to obliteration of all sorrows,
of life after life."

[Verse no. 33, Hanumān Chālisā,]

"यह शत बार पाठ कर जोई,
छूटहि बन्दि महासुख होई"

"Yaha shat baar pātha kar joī,
Chhootahi bandi mahāsukha hoī"

"One who recites this Hanumān Chālisā hundred times,
Free of all bondage shall he be,
Gaining infinitude of joys."

[Verse no. 38, Hanumān Chālisā][4]

We give here below a verse from Hanumānaṣhṭaka which explains how Hanumānji's grace can transform one's life. This goes as:

काज किये बड़ देवन के तुम,
वीर महाप्रभु देखि विचारो।।
कौन सो संकट मोर गरीब को,
जो तुमसो नहिं जात है टारो।।
वेगि हरो हनुमान महाप्रभु,
जो कछु संकट होय हमारो।।
को नहिं जानत है जग में कपि,
संकट मोचन नाम तिहारो।।

Kaaja kiye baḍa devana ke tum,
Veer Mahāprabhu dekhi vicharo,
Kaun so sankat mora gareeb ko,
Jo tumso nahi jaat hai taro,
Vegi haro Hanuman Mahaprabhu,
Jo kachhu sankat hoye hamaro,
Ko nahi jaanat hai jag mein kapi,
Sankat Mochan naam tiharo.

"Oh! Great hero! Oh! Supreme Lord!, Hanumānji
Major undertakings of gods have been carried out by you,
Please just think,
Can there be any difficulty,
Facing a lowly being like me,
which is beyond you;
Oh! Hanumānji, Oh! great Lord!
Whatever be the obstructions in our life,

Speedily make them vanish"
Who is not aware in this world,
Oh! Swami,
Your very moniker is,
Always a saviour in critical times"

[Verse no. 8]

If we thus chant Hanumān Chālisā regularly and if we have the good fortune to be blessed by Hanumānji, our worldly life will become totally carefree and full of joy. Not only this we will also attain the ultimate aim of human life which is to secure freedom the unending cycle of birth and death.

The last stanza of Hanumān Arti goes as:
"जो हनुमान जी की आरती गावै, बसि बैकुण्ठ परमपद पावै"

Jo Hanumānji ki aartī gavae,
Basi Baikunth paramapada pavae !

"One who sings the Arti of Hanumānji,
He will be established Vaikunth,
The Supreme Abode,
(Never to return again)"

An ordinary reader may not readily accept all this. He may argue that he is not bothered about life after death or salvation. But one thing is certain—if he reads Hanumān Chālisā with a sense of commitment everyday, he will be gradually influenced by it. **He will think twice before undertaking some unethical action or being disrespectful to his parents or elders. Would this be a small gain?**

There is another key aspect relating to Hanumān Chālīsā which needs to be kept in mind. It has been recorded on "YouTube," etc., by renowned singers. **But while listening to it, one should not be carried away by the musical intonations of singers or by the notes of accompanying musical instruments, however sweet and melodious. Hanumān Chālīsā should be listened to or read with one's heart rather than one's ears or eyes. One** should also thoroughly familiarize himself/herself with the meaning of its different verses by repeatedly reading its translation.

As you read or listen to Hanumān Chālīsā, various scenes from the Rāmāyana as portrayed in its verses must conjure up slowly before your eyes. This is the key to unlocking its benefits. A word or two here about the transliteration of various devotional hymns given in this tract would be in order. We have included it specially for foreigners and people of Indian origin abroad not familiar with Devanagari script. **We are sure even a cursary perusal of these transliterations will give their readers some sense of the fantastic melody, sweetness and rhythm of these emotive lyrics.**

We have now reached what is probably the most pleasant part of this preface, namely giving of credits. First of all, I would like to express my sincere thanks to Shri Abhishekji Jain, proprietor of M/s Motilal Banarasidass International for publishing this tract in such an attractive manner and getting it printed so quickly. In fact, it was he who suggested that I should bring out such a text, and I am most grateful to him for this suggestion.

I will also like to express my heartfelt thanks to their production manager, Ms. Poonamji Taneja, who has been unwavering in her commitment to this book and ensuring it gets printed to the highest standard. Pictures of Hanumānji in this book were obtained by her after painstaking search. I am always sure that I can count on her in every way, and she does her best to resolve whatever problems I might be facing.

Coming now to the actual compilation of this book the first name that comes to my mind is of my wife Nalini. She is very well acquainted with the Avadi language and has helped me greatly with its translation. Being familiar with Hindi grammar, she also explained to me some of the intricate points of grammar and how the poetry of Tulsidasji conforms to them rendering it more melodious.

When one brings out a book perhaps the most laborious and arduous task is that of typing it. Here, my unstinted thanks are due to Rituji Manchanda. She has been most enthusiastic about typing this manuscript, and has corrected it repeatedly without least annoyance. She has taken great interest in this project, and I much appreciate her enthusiastic support and constant backing.

My sincere thanks are also due to Ms. Vandanaji Eksambekar of M/s. Asmita Enterprises for typesetting this manuscript with her usual professionalism and expertise. Vandanaji has been working with me for the last several years and I consider myself fortunate that I have somebody like her to help me.

Finally, but not in the least, I would also like to acknowledge the role played by a young boy, no more than 11 or 12 years old, one named Ridham. He has learned Hanumān Chālisā from his Nani, and with great zeal recites it every night. He told me that whenever he faces any difficulty in his daily life, he thinks of Hanumānji and a surge of energy passes through him. Even when on a holiday abroad he does not forget to recite it. I truly learnt a lot from Ridham.

We tend to think that the younger generation in India is going astray from our traditions and heritage. We feel they act in a manner which is far from appropriate. However, from the commitment which Ridham shows to the recital of Hanumān Chālisā, I am convinced that many many young people today have a strong underpinning of ethics and morality.

If India is to rise, its resurgence will depend not merely on economic growth; it must side by side be able to abide by our traditional values and morality. I sincerely hold the view that there is a large section of young people in India who believe in God and who believe in observing the values which have been handed down to us by our parents and grandparents. It is not our constitutional provisions which will hold us together, but rather our traditions and moral values will act as a glue.

A society, however rich it may be, will surely degenerate unless it has the bulwark of eternal values. This has happened to other societies and the same fate will surely overtake India unless it firmly anchors itself to its past. Arnold Toynbee, the great historian, is on record as observing that most of the twenty civilizations that had perished during the last eight thousand years had no faith in God. India very much needs to protect itself from such a denouement. This can be achieved only by regular recital of sacred texts like Hanumān Chalisa with faith, devotion and understanding.

Finally, I would like to offer humbly a piece of advice for the people of India. **As a people we must learn to dream; but dream of what?** Not of course of merely earning more and more money or desperately trying to secure a H-1B visa to emigrate to the U.S.A. We are reminded here of the wise words of Joseph Weizenbaum : 'We can count but are rapidly forgetting how to say what is worth counting and why'.

We must dream of putting our country before our selfish interests so that it becomes "great" again in the widest sense of the word. Here we can do no better than turn to Hanumānji for inspiration who was totally selfless and lived solely to promote the cause of Dharma. Let us all try to emulate Hanumanji to the extent possible. I am sure if we do so we will certainly become the "Vishwa Guru" as we were in our pristine past.

The purpose of writing this book, publishing it, and getting it circulated both in India and abroad **is to spread God's word, acquaint the people with our ageless heritage and create in their minds the feeling that there is more to life than we understand, and that man is far more than his body.** With these thoughts, and seeking Hanumānji's blessings for all our readers, it is with great pleasure and humility that I lay this book before them.

Section I

Sri HANUMĀN CHĀLĪSĀ

(Tulasidāsji says)

श्री गुरु चरन सरोज रज ।
निज मनु मुकुरु सुधारि ॥
बरनउँ रघुवर बिमल जसु ।
जो दायकु फल चारि ॥

Śrī guru charaṇ saroj raja,
Nija manu mukur sudhāri,
Barnauṅ raghuvar vimala jasu,
Jo dāyaku phal chari

"As I undertake the portrayal,
Of Lord Rāma's sublime glory,
Which leads to fulfilment,
Of the four goals[5] of life,
(First) will I sanctify,
The mirror of my mind,
(Covered with sinful thoughts),
By the holy dust,
Of the lotus feet of my Guru."

बुद्धिहीन तनु जानिके ।
सुमिरौं पवन -कुमार ॥
बल बुद्धि विद्या देहु मोहिं ।
हरहु क्लेश विकार ॥

Budhihīna tanu jānike, sumiraun pawan-kumār,
Bal budhi vidya dehu mohin, harahu kalesh vikāār.

Oh! Son of the Wind-God,
You know how weak of body,
And bereft of intelligence,

---

[5]These four goals are: Adherence to righteousness, acquisition of wealth, fulfilment of appropriate worldly desires and finally salvation.

Am I;
(How can I then possibly describe the glory of Lord Rāma);
As I meditate upon you,
(Seeking your grace),
Grant me strength, intellect, and wisdom,
And destroy all the passions and mental turmoil of mine."

जय हनुमान ज्ञान गुन सागर ।
जय कपीस तिहुँ लोक उजागर ।।

Jai Hanumāna gyāna guna sāgara,
Jai kapīs tihun loka ujāāgara.

"Hail to Hanumānji, hail to Hanumānji,
The very ocean of wisdom and virtues,
Victory to the Lord of Monkeys,
Brightly shines your glory in all the three worlds,
The heaven, the earth and the netherworld;

[Verse No. 1]

रामदूत अतुलित बल धामा ।
अंजनि-पुत्र पवनसुत नामा ।।

Rāmdoot atulita baldhāmā,
Anjani-putra pawansuta nāmā.

The (acclaimed) messenger of Lord Rāma,
The repository of incomparable strength and power;
Known also as 'the son of Anjani', 'the son of the Wind-God'

[Verse No. 2]

महावीर विक्रम बजरंगी।
कुमति निवार सुमति के संगी ।।

"Mahāveera vikrama bajrangī,
Kumati niwaara sumati ke sangi"

"(Oh! Hanumānji, Oh! Lord-God!)

Foremost among heroes,
Acclaimed for your feats of valour,
With an adamantine body like a thunderbolt,
Stupendous of strength,
You erase the depravity of mind of your devotees,
(Endowing them with wisdom),
Being the unflinching ally of the wise and saints"

[Verse No. 3]

कंचन वरन विराज सुवेसा ।
कानन कुण्डल कुञ्चित केसा ।।

Kanchana varana virāāja suvesā,
Kānana kundala kunchita kesā

"Of golden hue, curly of hair,
Golden earrings dangling from your ears,
So attractive are your vestaments,
How very auspicious is your appearance."

[Verse No. 4]

हाथ बज्र औ ध्वजा विराजै ।
काँधे मूँज जनेउ साजै ।।

Hāatha bajra au dhwajā virajai
Kandle moonja janeu sājai

"(How magnificent are your looks!),
With a mace in your hand,
A flag fluttering in the other;
Embellishing the shoulder,
Being the sacred thread of long reed,
(Wrapped) around it;"

[Verse No. 5]

शंकर सुवन केसरी नन्दन ।
तेज प्रताप महा जग वन्दन ।।

Śankera suvana Kesari nandana,
Teja pratāpa mahā jaga vandana

Oh! Hanumānji, Oh! Embodiment of Bhagwan Śivaji,
Oh! Son of Lord Kesarī,
All the world pays obeisance,
To your indescribable splendour and unparalleled deeds of
valour."

[Verse No. 6]

विद्यावान गुणी अति चातुर ।
राम काज करिबे को आतुर ।।

Vidyāwāna gunī ati chātura,
Rāma kāja karibe ko ātura.

"(Oh! Hanumānji, Oh! Swami)
You are the one,
Well-versed in all branches of knowledge,
Repository of sterling virtues,
Most Sagacious,
Always yearning to carry out,
The missions of Lord Rāma,

[Verse No. 7]

प्रभु चरित्र सुनिबे को रसिया ।
राम लखन सीता मन बसिया ।।

Prabhu charitra sunibe ko rasiyā,
Rāmā Lakhana Sītā mana basiyā.

"Listening with great relish and exhilaration,
To the accomplishments of Lord Rāma,
(Being beloved of Sri Rāma, Laxmanji and Sitaji),
Verily enshrined in your heart,
Are they:"

[Verse No. 8]

सूक्ष्म रूप धरि सियहिं दिखावा ।
विकट रूप धरि लंक जरावा ।।

Sūkshma rūpa dhari Siyahin dikhāwā,
Vikata rūpa dhari Lanka jarāwā.

"Appearing before Sitā in a tiny form,
(So as to reassure her),
Assuming a horrendous shape,
While engaged in setting fire to Lanka."

[Verse No. 9]

भीम रूप धरि असुर संहारे ।
रामचन्द्र के काज संवारे ।।

Bheema rūpa dhari asura sanhāre,
Rāmchandra ke kaja sanvāre.

"Exhibiting massive and gigantic proportions,
As a demon slayer,
(Transforming yourself as the occasion demanded),
Fulfilling the tasks of Lord Rāma"

[Verse No. 10]

लाय संजीवन लखन जियाये ।
श्री रघुबीर हरषि उर लाये ।।

Lāya Sanjīvana Lakhana jiyāye,
Śrī Raghubīr haraṣi ura lāye.

"(With death hovering over Laxmanji,
Struck by a deadly arrow from Meghānandà),
Oh! Hanumānji! Oh! Great Hero!
(Only) by your bringing the Sanjivini plant[6],
(From the far away Himālayās),

---

[6] A unique life-restoring plant not found anywhere apart from distant Himālayās. Its extracts contained life-giving nectar.

The life of Laxmanji could be restored;
Being overjoyed,
Lord Rāma clasped you to his heart"

[Verse No. 11]

रघुपति कीन्हीं बहुत बड़ाई।
तुम मम प्रिय भरतहि सम भाई ।।

Raghupati kīnhī bahuta badhāī,
Tuma mama priya Bharatahi sama bhāī.

"Lavishly praising you Lord Rāma exclaimed:
Even as dear as my brother Bharat,
Are you to me."

[Verse No. 12]

सहस बदन तुम्हरो यश गावैं।
अस कहि श्रीपति कंठ लगावैं ।।

Sahasa Badana tumharo yasa gāvaīn,
Asa kahi Śrīpati kaṇṭh lagāvain.

Oh! Hanumānji,
Lord Rāma then held you to his heart,
Declared (jubilantly),
(So dazzling) is your success,
That (Shesh Nag) himself through his thousand mouths,
Will need to extol it."

[Verse No. 13]

सनकादिक ब्रह्मादि मुनीसा ।
नारद सारद सहित अहीसा ।।

Sanakādika Bramhādi Munīsā,
Nārada Sārada Sahit Ahīsā.

यम कुबेर दिगपाल जहाँ ते।
कवि कोविद कहि सके कहाँ ते ।।

46

Yama Kubera Digpāla jahān te,
Kavi kovida kahi sake kahān te.

"Sages like Śrisanak (Śrisanandan, Śri Sanat Kumar) and so on,
gods like Brahmaji, Naradji, Devi Saraswatiji, the Shesh Nag,
As well as, Yama, Kubera, guardians of directions and other celestial beings, wherever they may be,
Along with great poets and eminent scholars,
Even all such towering personalities,
Would be unable,
To duly describe the glory of your success."

[Verses no. 14, 15]

तुम उपकार सुग्रीवहिं कीन्हा।
राम मिलाय राजपद दीन्हा ।।

Tuma upkāra Sugrīvahin kīnhā,
Rāma milāya rāja pada dīnhā.

"Oh! Hanumānji! Oh! Mahatma,
It was due to your grace only,
That Sugrivji could meet Lord Rāma,
He was then anointed as the king of monkeys,
By The Lord"

[Verse no. 16]

तुम्हरो मन्त्र विभीषण माना ।
लंकेश्वर भये सब जग जाना ।।

Tumharo mantra Bibhīshan mānā,
Lankeśvara bhae saba jaga jānā.

"All the world knows,
It was you, Oh! Hanumānji,
That counselled Vibhishan, the younger brother of Rāvana,

Who accepted your advice;
(Only due to your sagacious counsel,
Was Vibhishan emboldened,
To seek the grace of Lord Rāma,
Though he was the arch enemy of Rāvana)
Crowned was he then
(By Lord Rāma),
As the king of Lankā"

[Verse No. 17]

जुग सहस्र योजन पर भानू।
लील्यो ताहि मधुर फल जानू ।।

**Juga sahasra yojana para bhānū,
Līlyo tāhi madhura phala jānū.**

**"(Exhibiting extraordinary prowess in your childhood itself),
Oh! Hanumānji, Oh! Swami!
Believing the bright orb of the sun,
To be a ripe fruit,
(You sprang towards it),
Swallowing it,
Though two thousand of yojanas[7] away;"**

[Verse No. 18]

प्रभु मुद्रिका मेलि मुख माहीं ।
जलधि लांघि गए अचरज नाहीं ।।

*Prabhu mudrikā meli mukha māhīn,
Jaladhi lānghi gaye acharaja nāhīn.*

**Is there any wonder,
Oh! Hanumānji
You crossed over the mighty ocean,
Holding Lord Rāma's signet-ring in your mouth,**

---

[7]A measurement of distance used in the times of Tulasidasji. It approximates 37 KMs. Evidently people then were ignorant of the real distance between the sun and the earth.

(For handing over to Sitāji as memento)."

[Verse No. 19]

दुर्गम काज जगत के जेते ।
सुगम अनुग्रह तुम्हरे तेते ।।

Durgama kāja jagata ke jete,
Sugama anugraha tumhare tete.

**"With your blessings, Oh! Hanumānji,
Whatever be the undertakings of the world,
However arduous and fraught with difficulties,
Smoothly will they be carried out."**

[Verse No. 20]

राम दुआरे तुम रखवारे ।
होत न आज्ञा बिनु पैसारे ।।

*Rāma duāre tuma rakhavāre,
Hota na ājñā binu paisāre.*

**"You are the one,
Oh! Hanumānji,
Guarding the entry,
Into the presence of Lord Rāma,
Without your permission,
None can approach him;"
(No one can obtain communion with Lord Rāma,
In the absence of your grace)**

[Verse no. 21]

सब सुख लहै तुम्हारी सरना।
तुम रक्षक काहू को डरना ।।

*Saba sukha lahai tumhārī saranā,
Tuma racchaka kāhū ko ḍaranā.*

"One who has you as the guardian,

49

Oh! Hanumānji! Oh! Mahatma,
What has he to fear then?
Under your protection,
All the pleasures and comforts of the world,
Would be his to enjoy"

[Verse No. 22]

आपन तेज सम्हारो आपै ।
तीनों लोक हाँक तें काँपै ।।

Āpana teja samhāro āpai,
Tīnon loka hānka ten kanpai.

"Such is the splendour of your radiance,
That none but you can encompass or control it,
(So immensely powerful are you),
A mere snort from you,
Makes the three worlds tremble with fear."

[Verse No. 23]

भूत पिशाच निकट नहीं आवै।
महाबीर जब नाम सुनावै ।।

Bhūta pisācha nikata nahim āvai,
Mahābīra jaba nāma sunāvai.

"Oh! Hanumānji, Oh! Great Hero,
Ghosts, goblins and evil entities,
Dare not approach,
From where is heard
The recital of your (glorious name)"

[Verse no. 24]

नासै रोग हरै सब पीरा ।
जपत निरंतर हनुमत बीरा ।।

Nāsai roga harai saba pīrā,
Japat nirantara Hanumata Bīrā,

50

"Oh Hanumānji, Oh! Supreme Hero,"
One who continuously meditates on your name,
He obtains immediate relief,
From all diseases and ailments,
With an end put to his sufferings"

[Verse No. 25]

संकट ते हनुमान छुड़ावै ।
मन क्रम वचन ध्यान जो लावै ।।

Saṁkaṭa ten Hanumāna chuḍāvai,
Mana krama bachana dhiyāna jo lāvai.

"One who keeps the mind,
Focused on you alone,
In action, speech and thought,
All his difficulties and obstacles,
Are eliminated by you,
Oh! Hanumānji."

[Verse No. 26]

सब पर राम तपस्वी राजा ।
तिन के काज सकल तुम साजा ।।

Saba para Rāma tapasvī rājā,
Tina ke kāja sakala tum sājā.

(Though) towering above all,
Is Lord Rāma, the Sage-King,
All his tasks were carried out,
To perfection by you,
Oh! Hanumānji."

[Verse No. 27]

और मनोरथ जो कोई लावै ।
सोई अमित जीवन फल पावै ।।

Aura manoratha jo Koī lāvai,

51

Soī amita jīvan phala pāvai.

"Whatever be the devotee's aspirations, hopes and wishes,
(Not only will they be fulfilled,
By your grace),
But he will enjoy the most wonderous reward of life,
(Freedom from the cycle of birth and death or salvation)"

[Verse No. 28]

चारों जुग प्रताप तुम्हारा ।
है परसिद्ध जगत उजियारा ।।

Chāron juga pratāpa tumbhārā,
Hai parasiddha jagata ujiyārā.

"Oh! Hanumānji, Oh! Magnificent Hero!
Reverberate through the four yugas[8],
The fame of your magnificent feats of valour,
Illuminating the world with their resplendence;

[Verse No. 29]

साधु सन्त के तुम रखवारे ।
असुर निकंदन राम दुलारे ।।

Sādhu santa ke tum rakhavāre,
Asura nikandan Rāma dulāre.

The guardian of sages and saints,
Are you;
Slayer of demons are you,
As well as the one,
Supremely beloved of Lord Rāma."

[Verse No. 30]

अष्ट सिद्धि नौ निधि के दाता ।
अस बर दीन जानकी माता ।।

---

[8]These four yugas are: Satya Yuga, Treta Yuga, Dwapara Yuga and Kali Yuga.

Aṣṭa siddhi nau nidhi ke dātā,
Asa bara Dīna Jānakī Mātā.

"Oh! Hanumānji, Oh! Mahatma,
Thanks to the boon,
Granted to you by Janaki Matāji,
You possess the capacity to grant to anybody.
Eight magical powers and nine reservoirs of wealth;

[Verse No. 31]

राम रसायन तुम्हरे पासा ।
सदा रहो रघुपति के दासा ॥

Rāma rasāyana tumhare pāsa,
Sadā raho Raghupati ke dāsā.

Oh! Hanumānji, Oh! Lord!
May you remain for all times to come,
The most humble devotee of Lord Rāma,
Endowed as you are,
With the elixir of unbounded love and absolute devotion,
For him"

[Verse No. 32]

तुम्हरे भजन राम को पावै ।
जनम जनम के दुख बिसरावै ॥

Tumhare bhajana Rāma ko pāvai,
Janama janama ke dukha bisarāvai.

"Oh! Hanumānji! Oh! Swami!
Worshipping you with absolute devotion,
One attains the blissful world of Sri Rāma;
Where there won't be even a trace,
Of one's sorrows of past lives"

[Verse No. 33]

अन्त काल रघुवर पुर जाई।
जहाँ जन्म हरि भक्त कहाई ।।

Anta kāla Raghuver pura jāī,
Jahāṁ janma Hari bhakta kahāī.

"When the end comes,
That devotee would go to the (eternal) abode of Lord Rāma,
Even if he were to get a rebirth,
He will come to be then known as a devotee of Lord Rāma"

[Verse No. 34]

और देवता चित्त न धरई।
हनुमत सेइ सर्व सुख करई ।।

Aura devatā chitta na dharaī,
Hanumata seī sarba sukha karaī

"(One who is engaged in your worship, Oh! Hanumānji!),
To him you grant all pleasures and boons,
No need for him,
To turn to some other deity,
Seeking benediction"

[Verse No. 35]

संकट कटै मिटे सब पीरा ।
जो सुमिरे हनुमत बलबीरा ।।

Sankata kaṭai miṭai saba pīrā,
Jo sumirai Hanumata Balabīrā.

"One who meditates upon you,
Oh! Hanumānji! Oh! magnificent hero,
Embodiment of power and strength,
(Smooth and fragrant becomes the path of his life),
With all its thorns extracted,
All calamities and dangers overcome"

[Verse no. 36]

जय जय जय हनुमान गोसाई।
कृपा करहु गुरुदेव की नाई ।।

Jai Jai Jai Hanumān gosāīṁ,
Krupā karahu Gurudeo kī nāīṁ.

"Victory, victory, victory to Hanumānji,
Oh! Mahatma,
Please bestow your grace on me,
Like a Guru showering blessings on his disciple"

[Verse no. 37]

यह शत बार पाठ कर जोई।
छूटहि बँदि महासुख होई ।।

Yaha shat bāra pāṭha karā joī,
Chhūṭahi baṁdī mahāsukha hoī.

Tulasidasji says "By the (mere) perusal hundred times,
Of Hanumān Chālisā,
One would be released from the fetters of worldly existence,
Reaching a state of supreme felicity."

[Verse No. 38]

जो यह पढ़ै हनुमान चालीसा ।
होय सिध्द साखी गौरीसा ॥

Jo yaha padhai Hanumān chālīsā,
Hoya siddha sākhī Gaurīsā.

"(Tulsīdāsji avows)
Lord Śiva is my witness[9],
Completely fulfilled would be the one,

---

[9] The immortal Chālisā has come down from Lord Śiva. So the belief goes. This is the Implication of Tulasidāsji's words: 'Śiva is my witness'. The verse points to the symbiotic bond between Śivaji and Hanumanji.

Who (regularly) reads Hanumān Chālisā"

[Verse no. 39]

तुलसीदास सदा हरि चेरा ।
कीजै नाथ हृदय मँह डेरा ॥

Tulasīdāsa sadā Hari cherā,
Kījai Nātha hṛdaya maham dehā.

'(Tulasidāsji entreating Hanumānji),
Myself (Tulasidās) being for ever,
A humble devotee of Bhagwan Rāma,
May you, Oh! Lord Rāma, dwell
(For all times),
In my heart"

[Verse No. 40]

पवनतनय संकट हरन ।
मंगल मूरति रूप ॥
राम लखन सीता सहित ।
हृदय बसहु सुर भूप ॥

Pavanatanaya Sankaṭ Haran,
Mangala Mūrati Rūpa,
Rāma Lakhana Sītā Sahita,
Hṛdaya Basahu Sura Bhūpa.

(Tulasidāsji's entreaty),
Oh! Son of wind-god, Oh! The Saviour in all difficulties,
Oh! auspicious of appearance!
"May you, (Hanumānji),
Along with Bhagwan Rāma, the
Lord of gods,
And Laxmanji and Sitaji,
Be enshrined (for ever),
In my heart."

An explanatory note on Hanumān Chālisā:
Its verse no. 21 says that without Hanumānji's approval nobody can get Lord Rāma's blessings. This is vividly reflected in the iconography of temple complexes. In big temples where there is a shrine of Lord Rāma as well as of Hanumānji, the latter always faces the former. This is a vivid imagery symbolizing how without Hanumānji's nod no worshipper can hope to propitiate Lord Rāma.

The magnificent new Rāma Janmabhoomi temple in Ayodhya has very much within its precincts a shrine of Hanumānji enabling him to thus remain Bhagwān Rāma's eternal doorkeeper. Moreover, significantly enough, about a kilometre away from this temple is an ancient temple of Hanumānji built around 10th century. This is known as "Hanumāngarhi".

Traditionally over the centuries worshippers first paid obeisance at Hanumāngarhi' temple before proceeding to the Rāma mandir at the site of Janmabhoomi.

All this makes us cautiously conclude that from earliest times Hindus firmly believed that the way to Lord Rāma's blessings is paved with Hanumānji's grace. This is what probably induced Tulsidāsji to compose the following memorable chaupai:

"राम दुआरे तुम रखवारे।
होत न आज्ञा बिनु पैसारे ।।"

You, Hanumānji, are the one,
Guarding the door of Lord Rāma's chamber,
Without your permission,
None can step in."

This faith remains as entrenched today as ever and the daily footfall at Hanumāngarhi runs into tens of thousands, it spikes to even fifty thousand on special days, surpassing occasionally the number of visitors to the main Rāma Mandir itself. Thus the modern pilgrim firmly believes that it would be sacrilege to to for a Darshan of Rāma Lalaa without first paying obeisance to Hanumānji.

Turning now to Verse No. 35. It basically asks the devotee to focus only on the adoration of Hanumānji and not to bother about other gods. This is because Hanumānji will ensure fulfilment of all his wishes. Citing this verse:

और देवता चित्त न धरई ।
हनुमत सेइ सर्व सुख करई ॥   No. 35

Here we are reminded of verse 7.23 of the Gita which looks upon Lord Krishna as the paramount deity. It declares that worship of other deities (apart from Krishna) is undertaken by people of limited understanding which only brings fruits that are not lasting. However, worshippers of Lord Krishna get supreme happiness through communion with him. This verse goes as:

"अन्तवत्तु फलं तेषां तद्भवत्यल्पमेधसाम्।
देवान्देवयजो यान्ति मद्भक्ता यान्ति मामपि॥'   [7.23]

"But people of immature understanding,
(Worshipping other gods),
Transient and passing become their rewards;
Devotees of various deities,
Go to them;
My (Lord Krishna's) devotees,
Very much come to Me (Lord Krishna),
(Thus attaining salvation)."

Finally, we look at verses no 38 and 39. They highlight the importance of regular perusal of Hanumān Chālisā and declare in the name of Śivaji that such a practice would lead to fulfilment of worldly desires of the devotee and ultimately to salvation.

Stanza 18.69 of the Gita proclaims that one who imparts to worshippers of Lord Krishna the teachings of the Gita, being most profound, will ultimately reach Lord Krishnā as a result of his overwhelming faith in Him. Furthermore, such a devotee is described in the next stanza 18.70 as the one who does what is most pleasing to Lord Krishnā in (this world). Moreover, he shall always remain dearest to him.

We thus see that there are many striking parallels between Hanumān Chālisā and the Gitā. These are great scriptures of Hinduism, of humanity, and we should follow both of them. We should turn to Hanumān Chālisā to overcome our fears and anxieties. We can count upon Hanumānji to destroy and eradicate the demons in our minds including fear of anxiety; having steadied ourselves we should turn to the Gita and try to follow the path prescribed in it to reach a state of equanimity and serenity so that worldly events even unsavoury won't unduly ruffle us.

Finally, to conclude: Hanumān Chālisā has very much stood the test of time during the last five hundred years or so. Where there is Hanumānji, there is Hanumān Chālisā. It has become a perennial source of inspiration and strength for Hindus providing them with an unfailing avenue to express their faith in Hanumānji, in the Absolute. So edifying is this text that the Chinmaya Mission which was established for cultural renaissance of Hindus through Vedantic teachings planned to chant Hanumān Chālisā to mark the 75th anniversary of its founding on 11.01.2026.

Section II

HANUMĀNAṢṬAKA

बाल समय रवि भक्षि लियो तब,
तीनहुँ लोक भयो अंधियारो।
ताहिसु त्रास भयो जग को,
यह संकट काहु सों जात न टारो ॥
देवन आनि करी विनती तब,
छाड़ि दियो रवि कष्ट निवारो।
को नहिं जानत है जग में कपि,
संकट मोचन नाम तिहारो ॥

bāla samaya ravi bhakṣi liyo taba,
Tīnahuṁ loka bhayo aṁdhiyāro,
tāhisu trāsa bhayo jaga ko,
yaha saṁkaṭa kāhu som jāta na ṭăro.
devana āni karī vinatī taba,
chhāḍi diyo ravi kaṣṭa nivāro,
ko nahīṁ jānata hai jaga meṁ kapi,
saṁkaṭa mocana nāma tihāro.

"Oh! Swami ! Oh! Hanumānji
In your childhood itself,
(Believing the bright sun,
To be a ripe fruit),
You swallowed it;
Frightened then became the three worlds,
Being plunged into darkness;
With nobody then knowing how to get over the catastrophe;
Entreated by gods,
You let go the sun's orb from your mouth,
Dispelling the fear of all;
Who does not know in this world,
Oh! Venerable god,
The mere utterance of your name,
Protects one from all scourges,
Shielding one from every misfortunes"

[Verse No. 1]

बालि की त्रास कपीस बसै गिरि,
जात महाप्रभु पंथ निहारो ।
चौकि महामुनि साप दियो तब
चाहिय कौन विचार विचारो ।।
कै द्विज रूप लिवाइ महाप्रभु
सो तुम दास के शोक निवारो।
को नहिं जानत है जग में कपि संकट मोचन नाम तिहारो ।।

bāli kī trāsa kapīsa basai giri,
jāta mahāprabhu paṁtha nihāro,
cauki mahāmuni sāpa diyo taba
cāhiya kauna vicāra vicāro.
kai dvija rūpa livāi mahāprabhu,
so tuma dāsa ke śoka nivāro,
ko nahīṁ jānata hai jaga meṁ kapi
saṁkaṭa mocana nāma tihāro

"Threatened and intimidated by Bali, Lord of the monkeys,
Sugriva, his younger brother,
Had taken refuge in a certain hill,
Where Bali could not go due to the curse of a sage;
Observing Lord Rāma approaching that hill,
Apprehensive became Sugriva,
(Not knowing who the strangers were);
To enquire about them,
Sugriva asked you, oh! Hanumānji,
(to approach them);
You, oh! Great Mahatma,
Disguised then as a Brahmin,
(Befriended Lord Rāma),
And brought him along with Laxmanji,
For a meeting with Sugriva;
In this way, you, the sagacious Mahatma,
Always obliterate the sorrows of your devotees;
Who does not know in this world,
The mere utterance of your name,
Protects one from all dangers,

Shielding him from every misfortune;"

[Verse No. 2]

अंगद के संग लेन गये सिय
खोजि कपीश यह बैन उचारो ।
जीवत ना बचिहौं हमसों जु
बिना सुधि लाइ इहाँ पग धारो॥
हेरि थके तट सिन्धु सबै तब लाइ
सिय सुधि प्राण उबारो।
को नहिं जानत है जग में कपि
संकट मोचन नाम तिहारो ॥

amgada ke samga lena gaye siya
khoji kapīśa yaha baina ucaro,
jīvata nā bachihon hamason ju
binā sudhi lāī iham paga dhāro.
heri thake taṭa sindhu sabai taba lāī
siya sudhi prāṇa ubāro,
ko nahīm jānata hai jaga mem kapi
samkaṭa mocana nāma tihāro.

A contingent of monkey warriors,
Among whom were Angad, the crown prince and
Hanumānji,
Were ordered to go all over and search for Sītāji,
With a stern admonition from Sugriva, the Lord of the
monkeys,
That their life will be forfeited,
In case they bring no news of Sītāji,
(Looking everywhere they marched and marched),
Finally reached the sea shore, wearied and tired,
Having nowhere found Sītāji
Thus fearing for their life,
(Recalling the harsh words of Sugriva);
(You, the Mahatma, reassured them then);
(And sprang across the vast ocean),
Bringing back news of Sītāji;
Thus saving the lives of all monkey companions,

Who doesn't know in this world, oh! Swami,
Mere utterance of your name,
Protects one from all calamities,
Shielding one from every misfortune"

[Verse No. 3]

रावण त्रास दई सिय को सब
राक्षसि सो कहि शोक निवारो।
ताहि समय हनुमान महाप्रभु
जाय महा रजनीचर मारो॥
चाहत सीय अशोक सो आगि सु
दै प्रभु मुद्रिका शोक निवारो।
को नहिं जानत है जग में कपि
संकट मोचन नाम तिहारो॥

rāvaṇna trāsa daī siya ko saba rākṣasi so kahi śoka nivāro,
tāhi samaya hanumāna mahāprabhu jāya mahārajanīcara
māro.
cāhata siya aśoka so āgi su daī prabhu mudrikā śoka nibāro,
ko nahīṁ jānata hai jaga meṁ kapi
saṁkaṭa mocana nāma tihāro.

"(Plunged into deepest melancholy was Sītāji),
Being tormented by Rāvana,
Through demonesses guarding her;
A certain demoness then (Trijata)
Restrained other demonesses from harassing Sitaji,
And assuaged her anguish,
(The reason being, you the Supreme Lord, had earlier
appeared in her dream,
Portending the death of Rāvana);
Oh! Hanumānji, Oh! great Mahatma,
You had at that time slain terrible demons,
(And them reached the Ashoka tree under which was Sītāji.);
(Being in utter desperation),
She entreated the Ashoka tree for fire,
(So she could end her life);
Only by your giving her the signet-ring of Lord Rāma,

63

She regained her composure;
Who doesn't know in this world,
Oh! Lord!
Mere utterance of your name,
Protects one from all dangers,
Shielding one from every misfortune."

[Verse No. 4]

बाण लग्यो उर लक्ष्मण के तब
प्राण तजे सुत रावण मारो।
लै गृह वैद्य सुषेण समेत.
तबहिं गिरि द्रोन सु वीर उबारो॥
आनि संजीवन हाथ दई तब
लक्ष्मण के तुम प्राण उबारो।
को नहिं जानत है जग में कपि
संकट मोचन नाम तिहारो॥

bāṇa lagyo ura lakṣmaṇa ke taba
prāṇa taje suta rāvaṇa maro,
lai graha vaidya Suṣeṇa sameta
tabahiṁ giri drona su vīra ubāro.
āni saṁjīvana hātha daī taba
lakṣmaṇa ke tuma prāṇa ubāro,
ko nahīṁ jānata hai jaga meṁ kapi
saṁkaṭa mocana nāma tihāro.

"Laxmanji was on the verge of death,
Being struck by a deadly arrow in his chest,
Launched by Indrajeet, the son of Rāvan;
From the entourage of Ravan himself,
You secretly spirited away Suṣeṇa,
(The renowned physician of Rāvana),
(And brought him over to Lord Rāma,
For ministering to Laxmanji,
Whose life was ticking away);
(As per the advice of suṣeṇa,
You flew to far-away Himālayās;)
And carried back in hand a giant mountain called Drona

64

On which fluttered Sanjivini.
The magical medicinal plant
With which was revived Laxmanji;
Who does not know in this world, oh! Mahatma!
The mere utterance of your name,
Protects one from all dangers,
Shielding one from every misfortune."

[Verse no. 5]

रावण युद्ध अजान कियो तब
नाग के फाँसि सबै सिर डारो।
श्री रघुनाथ समेत सबै दल
मोह भयो यह संकट भारो ॥
आनि खगेश तबै हनुमान जु
बन्धन काटि सुत्रास निवारो।
को नहिं जानत है जग में कपि
संकट मोचन नाम तिहारो॥

Rāvana yuddha ajāna kiyo taba
nāga ke phāṁsi sabai sira dāro,
śrī raghunātha sameta sabai dala
moha bhayo yaha saṁkaṭa bhāro.
āni khageśa tabai hanumāna ju
bandhana kāṭi sutrāsa nivāro,
ko nahīṁ jānata hai jaga meṁ kapi
saṁkaṭa mocana nāma tihāro.

"Totally immersed in ignorance,
Being Rāvana,
He challenged and declared war,
On Lord Rāma himself,
(Though no different from the Supreme Being);
(By Rāvan's powers of Maya),
Lord Rāma and his entire army,
Were shackled in lethal coils of serpents,
A terrible danger was confronting them then;
At that critical juncture,
You brought along with you 'Garud',

(the king of birds, and the arch enemy of serpents);
Garuda loosened the snake fetters,
Of Lord Rāma and his army.
Thus, Oh! Swāmi! you rescued them from an overwhelming
calamity;
Who doesn't know in this world, oh! the venerable
Mahatmā,
The mere utterance of your name,
Protects one from all dangers,
Shielding one from every misfortune!

[Verse No. 6]

बन्धु समेत जबै अहिरावण
लै रघुनाथ पाताल सिधारो।
देविहिं पूजि भली विधि सों बलि
देउ सबै मिलि मन्त्र विचारो ॥
जाई सहाई भयो तबहिं
अहिरावण सैन्य समेत सँहारो।
को नहिं जानत है जग में कपि
संकट मोचन नाम तिहारो॥

bandhu sameta jabai ahirāvaṇa
lei raghunātha pātāla sidhāro,
devihiṁ pūji bhāli vidhi soṁ bali
deu sabai mili mantra vicāro
jāī sahāī bhayo tabahim
ahirāvaṇa sainya sameta saṁhāro,
ko nahīṁ jānata hai jaga meṁ kapi
saṁkaṭa mocana nāma tihāro.

"When Ahirāwan had secretly carried to the nether world,
Lord Rāma and his brother Laxmanji,
Counselled was he by his demon companions,
To offer their sacrifice;
To their deity with all due rituals;
But at that juncture,
You went to the Netherworld to rescue them,
And destroyed Ahirāwan along with his army;

Who doesn't know in this world, oh! Swami,
The mere utterance of your name,
Protects one from all dangers,
Shielding one from every misfortune

[Verse No. 7]

काज किये बड़ देवन के तुम
वीर महाप्रभु देखि विचारो।
कौन सो संकट मोर गरीब को
जो तुम सो नहिं जात है टारो ॥
वेगि हरो हनुमान महाप्रभु
जो कछु संकट होई हमारो।
को नहिं जानत है जग में कपि
संकट मोचन नाम तिहारो॥

kāja kiye baRa devana ke tuma
vīra mahāprabhu dekhi vicāro,
kauna so saṁkaṭa mora garība ko
jo tuma so nahiṁ jāta hai ṭaro.
vegi haro hanumāna mahāprabhu
jo kachu saṁkaṭa hoī hamāro,
ko nahīṁ jānata hai jaga meṁ kapi
saṁkaṭa mocana nāma tihāro.

"Oh! Great Hero! Oh! Venerable Mahatma,
Many difficult tasks have been carried out by you,
Even of gods;
Just think of it, oh! Mahatma,
Can there possibly be a difficulty,
Confronting a weak and ordinary human being like me,
That you cannot resolve,
I pray, oh! Hanumānji, the Mahatma,
Quickly take away all the sufferings from my life;
Who does not know in this world, oh! Mahatama,
The mere utterance of your name,
Protects one from all dangers,
Shielding one from every misfortune"

[Verse no. 8]

67

लाल देह लाली लसे अरु धरि लाल लंगूर ।
बज्र देह दानव दलन जै जै जै कपि सूर ॥

lāla deha lālī lase aru dhari lāla laṁgūra,
bajra deha dānava dalana jai jai jai kapi sūra.

Oh! Hanumānji! Oh! God,
Red of body
Extremely hard like a missile
Anointed with crimson paste,
With a huge heavy tail,
Red in colour,
Destroyer of demons,
Epitome of courage,
"Hail, Hail to you" [Doha]

i) *'ṁ'* indicates nasal accent as well as 'n'.

ii) "C" is always pronounced as ch or च.

iii) Phrases and words have been added in the translation to bring out the meaning clearly.

Explanatory note on Hanumānaṣṭaka

In the last verse of this lyric Hanumānji is described as performing great tasks for deities which they evidently found difficult to carry out. In verse 11 of Bajrang Bāṇ Hanumānji's capabilities are held as surpassing those of all the deities put together. Citing from it:

"सुर समूह समरथ भटनागर"

Hanumānji's mace is always depicted as "वज्र" which signifies Indra's all-powerful thunderbolt which no adversary could resist. Thus Hanumānji is projected as equal to Indra, the lord of gods. To give two instance:

"हाथ बज्र औ ध्वजा विराजै"

Hanumān Chālisa (No. 5)

"बैरिहि मारू वज्र की कीले"

Bajrang Bāṇ (No. 12)

Hanumanji's splendour and radiance were overwhelming and even a snort from him sent the three worlds into a state of panic. Quoting from Hanumān Chālisa (no. 23)

"तीनों लोक हाँक ते काँपै"

All this should not surprise us as we know Hanumānji traces his lineage directly to Śivaji himself.

Can we conclude from all this that Hanumānji was the greatest deity? Here it would be futile to belabour this point further. We think comparisons of this kind which are relevant to our mortal world should not be literally applied to celestial beings.

Suffice to say Hanumānji's was a paramount and preeminent deity. Is it necessary to be more explicit?

BAJARANGBĀṆA

निश्चय प्रेम प्रतीति ते
Nishchaya prema prateeti te

विनय करे सन्मान
Vinay kare Sanmān

तेहि के कारज सकल शुभ
Tehi ke kāraja Sakala shubha

सिद्ध करैं हनुमान
Siddha karain Hanumān

"One who glorifies Hanumānji with humility,
Experiencing unwavering love and absolute faith towards him,
All of his tasks will be carried out to fruition,
By Hanumānji most auspiciously"

[DOHA 1]

जय हनुमंत संत हितकारी।
सुनि लीजै प्रभु अरज हमारी ॥ (1)

Jaya Hanumant sant hitkarī
Suni leeje prabhu araja hamari

"Victory be Hanumānji,
(Always) ensuring the welfare of sages and saints,
Oh! Lord!
please listen to our petition"

[Verse 1]

जन के काज विलम्ब न कीजै ।
आतुर दौरि महासुख दीजै ॥ (2)

Jana ke kāj vilamb na keejae
Aatur daun mahāsnkha deeje (2)

"Oh! Hanumānji!
please do not tarry,
In fulfilling the prayers of the devotees,
(Most earnestly they await your grace),
Rush here please,
Shower them with blessings and felicity."

[Verse 2]

जैसे कूदि सिन्धु माँहि पारा ।
सुरसा वदन पैठि विस्तारा ॥ (3)

Jaise koodi sindhu manhi parā
Sursā vadana paithi vistaarāa (3)

"Oh! Lord Hanumān,
As you were leaping across the ocean,
You entered the mouth of demoness Surasā[10],
Magnifying your body"

आगे जाइ लंकिनी रोका ।
मारेहु लात गई सुर लोका ॥ (4)

Aage jaai lankini roka
Mārehu laat gayi sur lokā

"Blocked you were as you traversed further (to Lankā),
By Lankinī (the demoness guardian of Lankā),
kicking her hard,
Consigned her to high heavens

[Verse 4]

जाइ विभीषण को सुख दीन्हा ।
सीता निरखि परम पद लीन्हा॥ (5)

---

[10] This is an allusion to a famous episode which occurred during Hanumānji's epic journey to Lankā.The demoness Surasā stood in his way with her mouth wide open. Hanumānji entered her mouth and exited through the other end.

Jai Vibhīshana ko sukh dīnha
Seeta nirakhi parama pada leenhā

"Meeting Vibhishan,[11]
(subsequently) which was to prove the cause,
of exceeding happiness for him;
By (being able to locate) and behold Sītāji
Oh! Lord Hanumān
You reached the topmost sacred place"

[Verse 5]

बाग उजारि सिन्धु मँह बोरा ।
अति आतुर यम कातर तोरा ।। (6)

Baag ujaari sindhu manha borā
Ati aatur Yama kaatar torā (6)

"You wrought destruction on (Ravana's) (beautiful) garden
(Ashoka Vatika),
Flinging into the sea,
The uprooted trees,
Being like the (veritable) Yama,
Frightening the demons,
Zestfully (slaughtering) them"

[Verse 6]

अक्षय कुमार को मारि संहारा ।
लूम लपेटि लंक को जारा ।। (7)

Akshaya Kumara ko maari sanharā,
Loom lapeti Lanka ko jārā (7)

---

[11] Hanumānji met Vibhishan for the first time when he had landed in Lankā in search of Sītā. Though Vibhishan was Rāvana's brother Hanumānji came to trust him. Subsequently, Lord Rāma on Hanumānji's advice unreservedly accepts Vibhishan as his friend and ally. Lord Rāma later appoints him as the king of Lankā. Thus, Hanumānji's meeting with Vibhishan was to prove the precursor of a very honourable and joyful life for the latter

"Destroyed Akshaya kumara (the son of Rāvana),
Burnt down Lankā,
By blazing rays around your tail;"

[Verse 7]

लाह समान लंक जरि गई ।
जय जय धुनि सुरपुर मँह भई ॥ (8)

Laah samaan lank jari gayi
Jaya jaya dhuni surpura manh bhai ॥ (8)

"Lankā was devoured (by fire),
As if made up of (highly inflammable) lāka,
"High heavens resounded with the chants of "Victory, victory to
Hanumānji"

[Verse 8]

अब विलम्ब केहि कारण स्वामी।
कृपा करो उर अन्तर्यामी ॥ (9)

Ab vilamb kehi kaaran Swamī
kripā karo ura antaryāmī ॥ (9)

"Oh! Master!
What is the cause now of any more delay,
(In coming to our succour),
You are the one,
Who knows very well,
What goes on in our mind"

[Verse 9]

जय जय लक्ष्मण प्राण के दाता ।
आतुर होइ दुख हरहु निपाता ॥ (10)

Jaya jaya Lakshmana pranuke dātā ।

Aātura hoi dukha harahu nipaataa ‖ (10)

"Hail, Hail to Hanumānji,
Being the one who granted[12]
A new lease of life to Laxmanji,
Anxious are we,
For you to appear,
To relieve us of our sorrows"

[Verse 10]

जै गिरिधर जै जै सुख सागर ।
सुर समूह समरथ भटनागर ॥

Jai Giridhara jai jai sukhsaagara

Sura samooha samaratha Bhatnaagara ‖ (11)

"Hail, Hail to Lord Hanumān,
Renowned as the one who bore aloft a huge mountain,[13]
Victory, victory to Hanumānji,
The ocean of bliss[14];
Rivalling the power and capabilities,
Of all the gods,
Put together"

[Verse 11]

ॐ हनु हनु हनुमन्त हठीले।
बैरिहि मारू बज्र की कीले ॥ (12)

Om hanu hanu Hanumant hatheele

bairihi maru bajra kī keele ‖ (12)

---

[12] Allusion to the Sanjīveeni plant brought by Hanumānji from distant
Himālayas to save the life of mortally–wounded Laxmanji.
[13] Reference to Hanumānji all by himself carrying a huge mountain on which
fluttered a Sanjeevini plant to revive Laxmanji who was near death
[14] Emphasizes Hanumānji's personality as a Gyani. A Supreme Gyani identifies
himself with Absolute which is nothing but bliss.

"Oh! Lord Hanumānji unshakable of resolve,
Slay the enemy,
By the hard projections of (your) mace"

[Verse 12]

गदा वज्र लै बैरिहि मारो।
महाराज प्रभु दास उबारो ॥ (13)

Gada vajra lai bairihi maro
Maharaj prabhu daas ubaaro (13)

"Oh! Lord, Oh! the Supreme Ruler,
With your thunderbolt[15] like mace,
Slaughter the enemy,
Give succour to this humble devotee"

[Verse 13]

ऊँकार हुँकार प्रभु धावो ।
वज्र गदा हनु विलम्ब न लावो ॥ (14)

Unkāra hunkāra prabhu dhaavo
Vajra gadaa hanu vilamb na laavo (14)

"Oh! Lord Hanumān,
Rush, Rush (here for our sake),
Snorting Huuṁ, Huuṁ Sonorously,
(Frightening the enemy),
Slaughter him with your thunderbolt[16] like mace,
Do not delay, Oh! Master,
(In coming to our rescue)"

[Verse 14]

ॐ हीं हीं हीं हनुमन्त कपीशा ।
ॐ हुँ हुँ हुँ हनु अरि उर शीशा ॥ (15)

---

[15] This was Indra's potent missile which was capable of killing any opponent. Hanumānji is portrayed as equal to Indra.

[16] Ibid.

Om hrīm hrīm hrīm Hanumānt kapeeshā
Om hum hum hum hanu ari ura sheeshā (15)

"Oh ! Hanumānt,
Oh! Lord of the monkeys,
Cut off the heads,
Of evil elements from their bodies"

[Verse 15]

सत्य होई हरि शपथ पाय के।
रामदूत धरू मारू जाय के ॥ (16)

Satya hoee Hari shapatha paay ke
Ramdoot dharu maaru jaaya ke (16)

Oh! Emissary of Lord Rāma,
Rush there, overpower the enemy and kill him,
Fulfilling the solemn assurance of Lord Rāma,
Truly this is what is going to happen."

[Verse 16]

जय जय जय हनुमन्त अगाधा ।
दुःख पावत जन केहि अपराधा ॥ (17)

Jaya jaya jaya Hanumant agaadhaa
Dukh paawata jana kehi aparaadhā (17)

Oh! Hanumānji!
The unbounded, the inconceivable, the unimaginable,
Hail to you, Hail to you, Hail to you!
What would be the crime,
Committed by these poor devotees of yours,
That they continue to suffer and suffer"

[Verse 17]

पूजा जप तप नेम अचारा ।
नहिं जानत हौं दास तुम्हारा ॥ (18)

Poojā japa tapa nema achaaraa
Nahin jaanat haun daas tumhaara (18)

"Bereft of knowledge,
Is this humble devotee of yours,
Of proper modes of worship,
Be they chanting, austerities, recital of holy names or ethical
norms"

[Verse 18]

वन उपवन मग गिरि गृह माहीं
तुम्हरे बल हम. डरपत नाहीं ॥ (19)

Vana upvana maga giri griha mahi
tumhare bala hama darpata nahi (19)

Fearless are we,
Being blessed with your grace,
Wherever we may be,
In forest, in garden, during travel,
On mountain top or at home"

[Verse 19]

पाँय परौं कर जोरि मनावौं
येहि अवसर अब केहि गोहरावौं (20)

Paay paraun kar jori manaavaun
Yehi awasara ab kehi gohraavaun (20)

"We propitiate you,
Falling at your feet,
Folding our hands in supplication;
At this juncture who else can be entreated for blessings"

[Verse 20]

जय अंजनी कुमार बलवन्ता ।
शंकर सुवन वीर हनुमन्ता ॥ (21)

Jaya Anjanee kumara balwantaa,
Shankara Suwana Veer Hanumāntaa (21)

"Victory to Hanumānji , the foremost hero !
The son of Anjanee,
Of stupendous strength,
Possessed of the splendour of Lord Śiva"

[Verse 21]

वदन कराल काल कुल घालक
रामसहाय सदा प्रति पालक ॥ (22)

Vadana karaala kaala kula ghaalaka,
Rama sahaya sadaa pratipaalaka (22)

"Oh! Lord Hanumānji!
Possessed of physique!
So huge and fearsome,
Slayer of the clan of evil-doers!
unflinching supporter of Lord Rāma
Unfailing protector of one and all"

[Verse 22]

भूत प्रेत पिशाच निशाचर ।
अग्नि बैताल काल मारी मर ॥ (23)

Bhoota preta pishaacha nishaachara,
Agri baitaal kaal maari mara (23)

Oh! Lord Hanumānji!
Ghosts, Corpses, Vampires, Goblins,
Witches, fire-emitting evil spirits!
Whosoever they be"

[Verse 23]

इन्हें मारू तोहे शपथ राम की।
राखु नाथ मरयाद नाम की ॥ (24)

78

Inhen maaru tohe shapatha Rāma kī
Rakhu naatha maryaad naama kī (24)

Kill them all,
This is the solemn pledge of Lord Rāma.
Oh! Master!
Let the glory of Lord Rāma
Be not tainted,
(By failing to eradicate the evil spirits)"

[Verse 24]

जनक सुता हरिदास कहावौ ।
ताकी शपथ विलम्ब न लावौ ॥ (25)

Janakasutaa Haridaas kahavau
Taakee shapatha vilamba na laavan (24)

"Renowned are you, Lord Hanumān,
As a great devotee of Sitaji and Bhagawān Rāma,
You are called upon in their name,
Do not tarry (in appearing here)
(and relieving us of our sufferings)"

[Verse 25]

जय जय जय धुनि होत अकाशा ।
सुमिरत होत दुःसह दुःख नाशा ॥ (26)

Jaya jaya jaya dhuni hota akhaasha
Sumirata hota duhsaha duhkha naashaa (26)

"Hail be Hanumānji;
Odes of your glory,
Resound high up in the skies,
Here recollection of you,
Erases even unbearable agony;"

[Verse 26]

चरण शरण कर जोरि मनावौं
यहि अवसर अब केहि गोहरावौं ॥ (27)

Charana sharana kara jori manavaun
Yehi awasara ab kehi gohraavaun (27)

"Oh! Lord! Praying to you, beseeching you,
By prostrating before you,
Folding hands in obeisance before you;
At this juncture,
To whom else,
Shall we turn to,
For refuge"

[Verse 27]

उठु उठु चलु तोहि राम दुहाई।
पाय परौं कर जोरि मनाई ॥ (28)

Uthu uthu chalu tohi Ram duhaai
Paya paraun karā jori manai (28)

"I appeal to you,
In the name of none else,
But Lord Rāma himself,
Please arise and rush here,
For our succour,
I beg for your grace,
Falling on your feet,
Supplicating humbly with folded hands"

[Verse 28]

ॐ चं चं चं चपल चलन्ता ।
ॐ हनु हनु हनु हनु हनुमन्ता ।। (२९)

Om chan chan chan chapala chalantaa,
Om hanu hanu hanu hanu Hanumantaa. (29)

Oh! Lord Hanumān, of unmatched valour and power,
How agile and quick movement are you,
I salute you again and again"

[Verse 29]

ॐ हं हं हाँक देत कपि चंचल ।
ॐ सं सं सहमि पराने खल दल ।। (30)

Om Om hum hum haank deta Kapi Chanchala
Om san san sahami paraane khaladala. (30)

Oh! Lord!
One who is ever so active,
The assembly of demons,
(Violently) trembling,
By your harsh snorts Hum, Hum, Hum,
(Terrifying their hearts)
Being overwhelmed with fear and fright"

[Verse 30]

अपने जन को तुरत उबारौ।
सुमिरत होय आनन्द हमारौ ।। (31)

Apane jana ko turata ubārāo
Sumirat hoya aananda hamaarāo (31)

"Oh! Lord Hanumān do not delay,
In coming to the rescue of your devotees,
Overjoyed we become,
By only turning our mind to you"

[Verse 31]

यह बजरंग बाण जेहि मारै
ताहि कहो फिर कौन उबारै ।। (32)

Yaha Bajranga baaṇ jehi maarai
Tahi Kaho phir Kaun ubaaras (32)

"Who can possibly save that evil one,
Who has been struck,
By this (potent) missile-like Bajranga Bāṇ"

[Verse 32]

पाठ करै बजरंग बाण की।
हनुमत रक्षा करै प्राण की ॥ (33)

Paatha karain Bajranga baaṇ kee
Hanumata raksha Karain praana kee (33)

Recite the verses of Bajranga Bāṇ regularly with devotion,
Be assured then,
Hanumānji would be there,
To protect your life against all dangers"

[Verse 33]

यह बजरंग बाण जो जापै।
ता ते भूत-प्रेत सब काँपै ॥ (34)

Yaha Bajranga baaṇa jo jaapai
Taa te bhoota preta saba kaanpai (34)

"Evil spirits, ghosts, corpses,
All tremble with fright in the presence of one,
Engaged in recital of Bajrang Baṇ"

[Verse 34]

धूप देय अरु जपै हमेशा।
ताके तन नहिं रहै कलेशा ॥ (35)

Dhoop deya aru japai hamesha.
Taa ke tana nahin rahai kaleshaa (35)

"Ritualistically recite Bajrang Baṇ daily,
And by burning incense, etc.,
Free of all cares
Bereft of all woe's
Shall your persona be"

[Verse 35]

प्रेम प्रतीतिहि कपि भजे
Prema prateetihi kapi bhaje

सदा धरे उर ध्यान,
Sadaa dhare ura dhyaana

तेहि के कारज सकल शुभ
Tehi ke kaaraj sakala shubha

सिद्ध करैं हनुमान
Siddha karain Hanumaan

*"Worship Lord Hanumān
Experiencing for him,
Overflowing love and attachment;
With the mind focused upon him,
Always be engaged in his meditation;
Hanumānji will thus ensure,
All your auspicious tasks and works,
Are carried out successfully,
In a salutary manner."*

(Doha)

Explanatory note on Bajrang Bāṇ

As the reader would readily observe Bajrang Bāṇ is an ode in adoration of Shri Hanumānji. Hanumān Chālīsā too glorifies Hanumānji. While these two lyrics are similar in essence, there is a certain difference between them.

In Hanumān Chālīsā Hanumānji's magnificent splendour is portrayed but he remains a somewhat distant figure. The devotee is in awe of him and seeks his blessings.

But, on the other hand, there is a certain kind of intimacy in Bajrang Bāṇ between the supplicant and Hanumānji. He directly addresses him and beseeches his grace. One does not find such a sentiment in Hanumān Chālīsā.

Thus in Bajrang Bāṇ Hanumānji is projected very much as a "personal God" whom a devotee can intimately approach. In the first Dohā itself of Bajrang Bāṇ, the devotee is called upon to worship Hanumānji with unwavering love. But in sharp contrast in the first Dohā of Hanumān Chālīsā, Tulsidāsji pleads for purification of his mind so that he would be able to appropriately set forth the majesty of Hanumānji.

We cite below three stanzas from Bajrang Bāṇ where Hanumānji appears as very much loving, personal God who is easily approachable. These stanzas are: No. 2, 9 and 20. We have quoted them below.

जन के काज विलम्ब न कीजै।
आतुर दौरि महासुख दीजै॥

(No. 2)

"Oh! Hanumānji!
Please do not tarry,
In fulfilling the prayers of the devotees,
(Earnestly they await your grace),
Rush here please,
Shower them with blessings and felicity."

(No. 2)

अब विलम्ब केहि कारण स्वामी
कृपा करो उर अन्तर्यामी॥

(No. 9)

"Oh Master
What is the cause now,
Of any further delay,
(In coming to our succour);
Bless us,
You are the one,
Who knows very well,
What goes on in our mind.

(No. 9)

"पाँय परौं कर जोरि मनावौं
येहि अवसर अब केहि गोहरावौं"

"We propitiate you,
Prostrating ourselves at your feet,
Folding our hands in supplication;
At this juncture,
Who else can be entreated,
For blessings"

Section IV

Hanumān Ārti : Hymns in glorification of Lord Hanumānji.

आरती कीजै हनुमान लला की ।
Aarati keeje Hanumān lalaa kee
दुष्ट दलन रघुनाथ कला की ॥
Duṣṭa dalan Raghunāth kalaa kee　　　　　*(1)*

"Recite ritualistically the praise of noble Hanumānji,
To pay homage to him[17],
The hero who knew,
Just like Lord Rāma,
How to bring about,
The destruction of the wicked."

　　　　　　　　　　　　　　[Verse No. 1]

जाके बल से गिरिवर काँपै ।
Jaa ke bal se girivar kanpei
रोग दोष जा के निकट न झाँकै ॥
Rog dosh jaa ke nikat na jhaankei　　　　　*(2)*

"He was the one,
Confronted with whose strength,
Trembled even the majestic Himālayās,
The Lord of mountains;
Warded off from his devotees,
Are diseases and pestilences,
Calamities and evils of every kind,[18]

---

[17]The ritual of Arati is carried out for invoking the grace of a deity. A sanctified plate is taken around clock-wise in the front of deity's image while hymns in its glorification are sung. The plate contains certain sacred materials as well as a small lighted wick lamp.

[18]This has reference to the following episode in the Ramayana: A potent missile hurled by Indrajit (Rāvana's son) at Laxmanji had mortally injured him.

(So overwhelming is his prowess).”

[Verse No. 2]

अंजनी पुत्र महा बलदाई ।
Anjanee putra maha baladaai

संतन के हित सदा सहाई ॥
Santan ke hit sadaa, sahaai (3)

“Oh! Lord Hanumānji,
The son of Anjani,
Blessed with stupendous power,
The unflinching ally of Saints and Sages,
For ever in their support.”

[Verse No. 3]

दे बीरा रघुनाथ पठाए ।
De Beeraa Raghunāth pathaaye

लंका जारि सिया सुधि लाए ॥
Lankaa jari Sıya sudhi laaye (4)

“It was none but Hanumānji, the great hero,
To whom Lord Rama had entrusted,
(The arduous undertaking of finding whereabouts of Sitāji),
Hanumānji came back with this information,
After having set fire to Lanka.”

[Verse No. 4]

His life was slowly ebbing away. There was only one way to save him; he needed an extract of the 'Sanjivini plant' which was found only on the Himālayās far away in the north. But it had to be brought within a short time in order to save Laxmanji's life. To all this seemed an impossibility.

But Hanumānji jumped all the way to Himālayās; he then tore off a section of it where this rarest of rare plant existed and carried that huge hill all the way to Lanka, thus saving Laxmanji. He managed to carry out this incredible feat in a few hours.

Hence it is said: 'The Himālayās trembled after experiencing Hanumānji's strength.'

87

लंका सौ कोटि समुद्र सी खाई ।
Lanka sao koti samudra sī khaai

जात पवनसुत बार न लाई ॥
Jaat Pawansuta baar na laai (5)

**"The son of Wind - God[19] Hanumānji,
In a single leap reaching Lanka,
Spanning the huge expanse exceeding million yojanas of the
sea,
So very deep being its ravines."**

[Verse No. 5]

लंका जारि असुर संहारे ।
Lankaa jāri asur sanhaare

सिया राम जी के काज संवारे ॥
Siya Rāma jee ke kāja Sanware (6)

**"Setting fire to Lanka,
Crushing multitudes of demons into dust,
(Arduous) missions of Lord Rāma and Sitāji,
Were carried out by you, Lord Hanumānji,
(With utmost speed and ease)"**

[Verse No. 6]

लक्ष्मण मूर्छित पड़े सकारे ।
Lakshmaṇ moorchhita paḍe sakaare

आनि संजीवन प्राण उबारे ॥
Aani Sanjeevan praan ubaare (7)

"While Laxmanji was lying unconscious,

---

[19] Wind serves the people constantly without any interruption. This is how Hanumānji also engaged in selfless service. This is why Swami Tejomayānanda of Chinmaya Mission has described Hanumānji as an epitome of "ideal service"

(With death hovering over him),
(In an astounding feat),
(You Hanumānji by a giant leap,
Reached the distant Himālayās),
And returned at dawn itself
(Carrying the huge Himālayān hill),
On which fluttered the divine Sanjivini plant,
Giving a new lease of life to Laxmanji"

[Verse No. 7]

पैठि पाताल तोरि जम कारे ।
Paithi paataal tori jam kaare

अहिरावन की भुजा उखारे ॥
AhiRāvana *kee bhijna ukhaare*   (8)

Oh! Hanumānji,
"Penetrating the dark depths of the netherworld,
Tearing down the walls of the prison of Yama, the god of
death,
By you were ripped off,
The arms of demon AhiRāvan,
(Thus rescuing Lord Rāma and Laxmanji from their evil
clutches.)

[Verse No. 8]

बायें भुजा असुरदल मारे ।
Baayen bhujaa asur dal maare

दहिने भुजा सन्तजन तारे ॥
Dahine bhujaa santajana taare   (9)

"Slaying the multitudes of demons by your left hand,
By your right hand,
Protecting and glorifying the community of sages,
Is noble Hanumānji."

[Verse No. 9]

सुर नर मुनि आरती उतारे ।
Sur nar muni aaratee utaare

जय जय जय हनुमान उचारे ॥
Jai jai jai Hanumaan uchaare   (10)

**"The ritualistic worship of Hanumānji (Āarti),
Is performed by all,
Gods, men and sages;
Hailing the ever victorious Hanumānji."**

[Verse No. 10]

कंचन थार कपूर लौ छाई ।
Kanchan thaar kapoor lau chhaayi

आरती करत अंजना माई ॥
Aarati karat Anjanaa maayi   (11)

**"Mother Anjani is blessing Hanumānji,
Performing his Āarti,
Rotating in front of his face,
A golden thali,
On which kapūra[20] glows brightly!"**

[Verse No. 11]

जो हनुमान जी की आरती गावै ।
Jo Hanumān jee kee aarati gavai
बसि बैकुंठ परमपद पावै ॥
Basi baikuntha parampada paavai   (12)

"One who recites this Āarti of Hanumānji,
(Full of devotion and faith),
Certainly, Vaikunth, the supreme abode of Lord Vishnu,
Would become his final resting place."

[Verse No. 12]

---

[20]kapūra is used during religious rites. It burns brightly and quickly.

Concluding remarks:

From 15th to 18th century the Bhakti (devotional) movement flourished in India, especially in its northern and eastern regions. Apart from Goswāmi Tulsidāsji (1511 to 1623), this era also saw the emergence of a number of poet saints like Meerābāi, Surdās, Tukārām, etc., who extensively composed devotional lyrics expressing their love and adoration for Lord Krishna, Vitthal and so on. They portrayed the deity being worshipped in different manifestations such as a child, a loving personality, etc. Therefore one does not find any uniform characterization of the deity being glorified in their lyrics.

But, on the other hand, in the case of Tulasidāsji's hymns like Hanumān Chālisa, Bajrang Bāṇ, Hanumānaṣṭaka, etc., which we have reviewed earlier, the patron-deity is always the same: the redoubtable Hanumān, the heroic warrior, unrivalled in strength, always focused on destroying demons or evil elements. **All the hymns of Tulsidāsji including even Ārti, are therefore suffused with Veer Ras (the spirit of a great fighter). This feature is absent in the devotional hymns of other poet-saints. This is why like the resonant cry 'Jai Sri Rāma' Hanumān Chālisa too has become a symbol of the vibrant and resurgent Hinduism of modern times. It is therefore regularly chanted by R.S.S. Shakhas.**

To understand how Hanumānji is perceived in modern times we need to look at the seminal role played by Samarth Rāmdās (1608-1681) in disseminating the cult of his worship and projecting him as a warrior deity. Samarth Rāmdās was a Guru of Shivaji Mahārāj and fully supported him in his fight against the Moghul rule. The cave temple of Shivatharghal in Maharashtra where Swami Rāmdās had visions of Lord Rāma and Hanumānji has become a popular pilgrim destination.

In the neighbouring region Swamiji was to set up eleven temples dedicated to Hanumānji. All that area which now

forms a part of districts Satara, Kolhapur, etc. then belonged to the Kingdom of Shivaji Maharaj. In paeans composed expressing adoration of Hanumānji. Swamiji focused on his huge physique, tremendous strength and overwhelming prowess in battle. Swamiji wanted the local Hindus to fearlessly resist the Moghul soldiers. He exhorted the youth to become strong physically drawing inspiration from Hanumānji; he promoted 'Suryanamaskar' or 'Salutation to the Sun' as an ideal exercize for the youth.

Hanumānji contined to inspire people during subsequent centuries. In 1897 in Pune three young revolutionaries (Chafekar Brothers) shot dead a British official, one Walter Rand, the plague commissioner, for his atrocious conduct especially towards women, during the plague epidemic. They did so after taking a vow at a Hanumān temple.

Today the Indian society is intensely patriotic as seen from the tremendous popularity of war movies. Hanumānji therefore with his radiant warrior spirit can truly be taken as a mascot of muscular and self-assertive Hinduism of present times.

While a great fighter Hanumānji was totally free of Tamasic inclinations which degrade a human being, and lead him towards vice and evil. Along with his crusading zeal he was crystal pure and bereft of any demeaning passions.

Let us therefore try to be pure-minded like Hanumānji. He found a neckless of priceless gems worthless because within them there was no image of Lord Rāma. We should thus imbibe the lesson from Hanumānji that material acquisitions cannot be the means to man's spiritual growth. But unfortunately monetary greed unfettered by ethics has become the bane of the modern society, be it in India or elsewhere. By meditating on Hanumānji we should try to get over this demonic obsession of the modern man which will spell doom for him. But all this does not mean we should be unconcerned with worldly affairs. We should always staunchly oppose injustice and oppression in every possible way. We should also endeavour to perform our bounden duties in the best possible way, free of any anxiety, for promotion of public weal and above all for the upliftment of our immortal Soul.

Jai Jai Hanumān

<u>About the Author</u>

Dr. Prakash Joshi joined the Indian Foreign Service in early 1970s. He went on to hold various senior positions with distinction in different parts of the world, including the Gulf region, Africa, Europe, the Caribbean, etc., While posted to Guyana, South America as High Commissioner, he delivered on their TV network discourses on the Gita for over two years.

Dr. Prakash Joshi was educated in Cambridge, Gonville and Caius College, U.K. where he did Tripos in Mathematics. He had earlier graduated with high honours from the University of Bombay specializing in Mathematics. He was then nominated as a National Scholar and was awarded the prestigious Tata Scholarship for higher Education of Indians. During 1980s while posted in Delhi he completed his doctorate through the Jawaharlal Nehru University in the field of International Relations. He also qualified at that time as Interpreter in Arabic through the school of Foreign Languages, New Delhi. Dr.Prakash Joshi possesses an excellent knowledge of Sanskrit, and has a distinguished family background. His father Dr. V.M. Joshi, I.C.S., D.sc. was a renowned statistician.

Dr. Prakash Joshi has several publications to his credit in the field of Hindu metaphysics. These include

1. Saga of Hinduism - Volumes I and II: M.D. Publications, New Delhi.

2. Introduction to Sankara's Advaitism: Motilal Banarasidass Publishers, New Delhi. Revised Edition: published by Motilal Banarsidass International, Delhi.

3. Path to Liberation from known to unknown: Motilal Banarasidass Publishers, New Delhi, Revised edition published by Motilal Banarasidass International, Delhi.

4. From Vedanta to Modern Science: Ocean Books Pvt. Ltd. New Delhi.

5. Present Day Gita – a way of life: Publisher K.L. Ganju, New Delhi.

6. The Golden Decade 2005-2015, My life as Hony. Consul General: Publisher K.L. Ganju, New Delhi.

7. The glory of Vedic mathematics: Beating the computer. Published by M/s Motilal Banarasidass International, Delhi

8. The Saga of Hanumān: The universally venerated deity. Published by M/s Motilal Banarasidass International, Delhi

Dr. Prakash Joshi is also engaged in systematically translating Sanskrit classics into English. His published works are:

9. Translation of Shākuntalam into English: Publisher: Somanath Sanskrit University.

10. Translation of MudrāRākshasam into English: Publisher: Somanath Sanskrit University.

11. Translation of Meghadūtam into English. Published by M/s Motilal Banarasidass International, Delhi.

Forthcoming translations by the author of Sanskrit classics into English are :

12. Mālavikāgnimitram.

13. Vikramōrvaśīyam.

14. Ṛtusaṃhāra

15. Raghuvaṃśa (First five sargas)

Dr. Prakash Joshi thus hopes to translate into English all the main works of Mahākavi Kalidās.

His forthcoming publications by Motilal Banarasidass International being:

16. The hidden treasures of the Gita.

17. Quest: My Spiritual journey – in search of happiness [volumes I and II]

18. Translation of Sunderkānd into English.

19. Translation of Kalipujā into English.

Future publications of the author

20. A concise commentary on the Gita: original verses with transliteration. Extensive quotations from Gyaneshwari and Sri Sri Paramahansa Yogānanda.

21. Main themes of the Gita - its essence: original verses with transliteration along with English translation.

22. From plato to the Gita: similarity between ancient Greek and Indian philosophies.

Dr. Prakash Joshi was honoured with the prestigious J.P. International Award for special and outstanding contribution in the field of education in December, 2024.

Hanumānji with Lord Rāma and Śivaji